# The
# I-Quit-
# Smoking
# Diet

# The I-Quit-Smoking Diet

Janice Alpert, M.A.

CB
CONTEMPORARY
BOOKS
CHICAGO · NEW YORK

**Library of Congress Cataloging-in-Publication Data**

Alpert, Janice.
    The I-quit-smoking diet : the revolutionary 21 day plan that lets you stop smoking without gaining weight / Janice Alpert.
        p.    cm.
    Bibliography: p.
    ISBN 0-8092-4587-6 : $16.95
    1. Reducing diets.    2. Smoking.    3. Cigarette habit.    I. Title.
RM222.2.A396    1988
613.2′5—dc 19                                                    88-11718
                                                                    CIP

Published by Contemporary Books, Inc.
180 North Michigan Avenue, Chicago, Illinois 60601
Manufactured in the United States of America
Library of Congress Catalog Card Number: 88-11718
International Standard Book Number: 0-8092-4587-6

Published simultaneously in Canada by Beaverbooks, Ltd.
195 Allstate Parkway, Valleywood Business Park
Markham, Ontario L3R 4T8 Canada

To four people who,
though many years apart,
are forever in my heart:
my beloved parents
and
my beautiful children

# Contents

# Foreword

It is refreshing to pick up a self-help book that deals with the complex phenomenon of behavior change in a holistic manner. Too many books have espoused a simplistic approach, which ultimately can only lead the reader to frustration and disillusionment. In *The I-Quit-Smoking Diet*, Janice Alpert has taken a multidimensional approach to helping individuals control their eating habits. The program is broken down into progressive steps, which are easy to follow, theoretically sound, and integrate mental, physical, and emotional needs.

The author addresses the behavioral, emotional, and physiological components that the individual must change in order to succeed at keeping weight down after the termination of smoking. She suggests behavioral techniques that will help the ex-smoker to combat the stimuli that entice him or her to light up a cigarette or eat food. Many self-help books stop here. This book, however, takes the next step in a treatment strategy that goes to the core of the issue. It addresses the causes of the problem by taking the reader to the emotional component.

An excellent section discusses how the recent non-smoker can get in touch with the repressed and denied feelings that have caused emotional involvement with cigarettes and, later, food. A clear, step-by-step approach helps readers identify the many feelings that influence their desire to overeat. Going still another step, the author provides readers with a concise method for understanding the unmet inner needs that precipitate the feelings. Practical suggestions are offered on how to satisfy emotional needs in more productive ways than by smoking or eating.

To complete the holistic approach, Ms. Alpert next addresses the physiological component. She provides readers with an extensive section on dieting, exercise, and relaxation techniques. The suggested programs in each of these areas make the integration of dieting and exercise into one's daily life both realistic and practical.

Individuals who follow the program outlined in this book will not only gain control over a behavior they wish to change, but will also have empowered themselves with an awareness of feelings that lead to self-understanding. Using the concepts and exercises presented in this book will help you acquire a more complete understanding of yourself. Through self-insight comes empowerment to create the life you envision. Have fun expanding your inner self while improving your outer appearances. Less is more!

—John R. Martins, Ph.D.
Professor of Counseling
Roosevelt University
Chicago, Illinois

# Preface

Whenever I read a book, especially a self-help one, I am curious about the author. I want to know who the author is and why he or she wrote this book. So I thought it was only right that I share that information with you.

Professionally, my background is in individual, family, and group counseling. I have been in private practice for seven years. Through my counseling center, I see clients individually and with their families as well as give seminars and lead groups. I am also on staff part-time as a psychology instructor at a local community college. But my predominant focus is on dealing with victims of eating disorders; this includes treating compulsive overeaters, people of normal weight who think they are overweight, anorexics, bulimics, yo-yo dieters, and people who have quit smoking and subsequently gain unwanted weight.

I chose this area as my specialty for a very personal reason. Twelve years ago, I had an emotional eating problem. I was what I call a "professional dieter." I knew everything about what I should and should not eat, yet I could never stick to any long-term diet. I spent a tremendous amount of time and energy thinking about food, worrying about my weight, and searching for the latest ultimate fad diet that would surely cure my "weight" problem. Though I would lose some weight on these miracle programs, I inevitably regained it. And I was not very happy.

After realizing that my problem was much more involved than finding a new "diet," I went for some help. I am pleased to report that not only did I learn a great deal about myself, but my weight finally came off, and this time *permanently*. In conjunction with getting my act together and resolving my "weight" issues, I returned to school and completed my master's degree. It was then I decided to open up a private practice and specialize in eating problems. I wanted to combine my personal experience with my professional expertise in order to assist others.

In the course of the last seven years, I have seen and heard a great deal. But I continually found one theme repeating itself. Many of my clients who wanted to lose weight complained that their latest weight gain occurred shortly after they quit smoking. I decided I needed to do some research on this phenomenon. What I found, along with my own concepts on the emotional power of food plus a healthy, livable eating and activity plan, is what follows. As I think you will see, *Quitting smoking and gaining weight do not have to be synonymous!*

I truly enjoyed putting all this together. I wish you the best of luck and hope you find this book a helpful and beneficial tool. Change is not always easy, but it can be done.

—Janice Alpert, M.A.

# Acknowledgments

Every author has a "few" people to acknowledge, and I am no different. The first two people I want to thank are my editors, Shari Lesser Wenk and Susan Buntrock. Shari has been fabulous in her support and encouragement. I truly thank her for giving me the opportunity to share my ideas with the public. Susan has been a constant stabilizing and informative contact. Her calm reassurance was always appreciated.

Next I want to thank Susan Jaquith for assisting me in putting together the *I-Quit-Smoking Diet* eating plan. Her expertise in nutrition, along with her dedication to helping others, helped me tremendously. I would like to thank Holly Jamison, M.S., for helping me put together an activity plan that most people will be able to incorporate into their lives. Her experience is abundant, as is her enthusiasm and positive attitude toward life.

I also want to thank Iris Schy for her assistance in

typing and retyping this manuscript. That she was able to decipher what I presented her is a trait worth accolades.

Finally, I want to thank my dear friends and wonderful family for all their support and caring throughout my endeavors. They are too many to name, but they know who they are.

And to you, I say good luck! I hope you find this book an important and helpful step on your journey through life.

# Introduction

If you are reading this book, you probably have already quit smoking, or else you are certainly contemplating doing so. Well, good for you! For this book is not about convincing you to quit. It doesn't use scare tactics. You do not need me to tell you that smokers have lungs that are filled with dust and carbon monoxide and are as black as coal. You do not need me to point out that you may contract emphysema and be forced to wear an oxygen mask and look like a suited-up astronaut! You do not need me to remind you that if you are a heavy smoker, you may drop dead of a heart attack before the end of this sentence. Since this is not a book about scare tactics and we both know they are pointless, I would never dream of mentioning them!

The purpose of this book is to alleviate your worst fear about giving up smoking. This fear is usually more intense than the fear of cancer, bronchial disease, heart problems, or even death. This fear overrides well-known positives about quitting, such as living longer, feeling much healthier, having more stamina, and even having whiter teeth. None of these benefits seem to matter as much as the all-encompassing terror of weight gain. It is this fear that the *I-Quit-Smoking Diet* addresses and tries to ease.

As mentioned in the preface, I am a psychotherapist who specializes in the emotional aspects of overeating. Over the years, many of my clients have come to disclose their history of weight problems. Before long, I began to notice they shared one pattern of behavior. They would start off by saying something like this: "My weight has always been a problem. Usually, I would be up and down and up and down. But it didn't start getting really bad until I quit smoking. I just keep eating. I cannot seem to control myself. The most frustrating and confusing part is that I don't just eat when I am physically hungry, and usually the food doesn't even taste good! What in the world is wrong with me?" These people eat without much thinking, with hunger rarely present and taste being rather insignificant. No wonder they are upset!

It soon became clear to me that the weight gain so commonly considered to be due to metabolic change (more about that later) was really not what the extra pounds were indicating. The higher number on the scale came about when these people engaged in a lot of uncontrolled eating. They were substituting food for smoking.

The answer to this dilemma was not simply to suggest another new diet and exercise plan. Most of these people were already walking, talking caloric dictionaries and self-taught nutritionists, as well as exercise aficionados. The answer instead seemed to be to offer them a new and better understanding of how and why they had been using cigarettes, and how and why they were now beginning to use food in a similar manner. In addition to this better understanding, they also needed some new how-tos to help them permanently overcome their attachment to food.

Throughout my practice, and now throughout this book, that is precisely what I offer. I will be giving you new ideas, new perceptions, new techniques, and even a new eating (not "diet") plan and activity (not "exercise") plan. All of these are specifically designed to make the path from being a smoker to being an ex-smoker as smooth as possible—and you'll get a svelte body as part of the deal!

This book is organized in a step-by-step manner. When I read a self-help book, I like to skim it, read ahead, and jump around, but reading this one from cover to cover will increase your chances for a more successful experience. So good luck, and let us begin the changing process!

# 1
# A Word About Change

Successful dieting is part of an overall process of change. But before you can start changing, you need to consider what that process involves. Unlike so many self-help books that start off with a big pep talk on how great everything is going to be and how it's all smooth sailing ahead, this one discusses openly and honestly what occurs when human beings contemplate change.

Change starts with your vision of yourself. You have unlimited potential for being anything you want to be. No doubt, you've heard stories about people who overcome terrible situations: poor people who become millionaires; uneducated people who put themselves through school and become doctors, lawyers, and presidents; and even handicapped people who become Academy Award winners. How do these people make these unbelievable changes? By listening to their own inner voices or gut instincts.

We all have the ability to hear our own advice, but

1

often we ignore it. Your inner voice has been telling you to quit smoking for years, hasn't it? Thank goodness you are finally listening! You've made up a bunch of rationalizations and therefore have avoided a change that in the long run you know will be good for you. Some common excuses for continuing to smoke are: "I'll be cranky if I quit." "What will I do with my hands?" "I can't have a cup of coffee and really enjoy it without a cigarette." "If I quit, I will gain weight." But even with all these great "but ifs," your inner voice persists.

You can take control of your habits by listening to your inner voice when it tells you that you can change. Of course, change is not always easy. We generally prefer the familiar and the known to the unfamiliar and the unknown. You may have friends or relatives who are in unpleasant marriages or jobs but continue to stay in them to avoid the fear of the unknown and to hold on to the security of the known. Even if it *is* miserable, at least it is predictable misery. But if you believe that something inside you knows what is right for you, your innate fear of the unknown becomes less intense. This is not to say that you won't experience concern and should throw caution to the wind. Your inner self, which is there to protect as well as to guide, would never allow that. But caution combined with inner trust allows change to develop in a much easier, less anxious manner.

A less anxious and positive manner does not mean sitting by quietly and listening to this inner voice until change miraculously occurs. You will have to be an active participant. For example, if your inner voice said, "Go back to school," and you did but were negligent about doing your homework, studying for tests, or completing papers, a degree would not come your way very quickly. Getting in touch with and listening to your inner voice is really just the beginning. You need to be prepared to take action with this new insight. You need to be ready to pay attention to how you want to better your life. You have already embarked on that process by starting this book. But reading this book is only the first step.

Change requires patience. In the United States, most of us are used to "the quick fix." We want and like immediate gratification. We see something in the store and think, "Gee, I can't afford it until next year. Oh, what the heck, I'll charge it!" We are raised and conditioned not to wait. Patience is rarely seen as a virtuous trait.

Waiting and patience usually reap the highest rewards. When you smoked, whatever was happening, the smoking made it better. It helped alleviate any discomfort and enhanced the pleasurable. However, this too was immediate gratification. Food can also be a shortcut to avoiding discomfort. Patience can be more tiresome than getting the quick fix, but in the long run it is more satisfying. Most likely, you already know this fact. Your inner voice has probably been telling you this for years.

The bottom line is this: if you want permanent results, you must expend attention and effort. There is no doubt about it; you can do it. The key word is *you*. This book won't make you eat properly; you have to do it. So often ex-smokers say the *diet* worked but then *it* stopped. But if the diet worked, the reason was that they were following it. *It* stopped working only when *they* stopped working.

Take a moment and sit quietly and try to listen to your own inner voice. Some of the ideas here are making sense, I hope. Change does not have to be brutal or agonizing, but it usually does require some commitment and effort. Think about when you were learning to drive. You probably felt excited, anxious, and apprehensive. But you also felt that being able to drive was worth whatever discomfort you experienced in the short run.

When you quit smoking, there is always some discomfort. People often tend to turn to food as a substitute. Changing this pattern will not be totally comfortable or easy, but this book along with your inner voice, will make it as painless as possible and even try to help you have some fun. Whatever the discomfort, one thing is for sure: the discomfort will be very short, and in the long run you will feel and look marvelous. By the time you finish this book, quitting smoking and gaining weight will not seem to be synonymous. This book will provide you with the foundation to ensure that the quitting process is a smooth one. It is up to you to build from there. Good luck!

# 2
# Arming Yourself with Knowledge: The Physiological Effects of Quitting

No doubt, you have heard horror stories about ex-smokers and what happens to them when they quit. Besides experiencing all kinds of withdrawal symptoms, some of them eat and eat and eat, putting on 5, 10, 20 pounds, or even more. But quitting doesn't have to make you fat, not if you know what to expect. Knowledge about smoking and quitting should make you less afraid of quitting and also more prepared to keep from replacing smoking with other destructive behaviors such as overeating.

To understand what happens to your body when you quit, you need to understand what smoking does to your body. First, consider what happens when you inhale. When you smoke, you inhale quite a variety of chemicals. The most common are tar, carbon monoxide, and nicotine.

Tar is not addictive, just poisonous. According to the American Lung Association (ALA), tar is the chemical most linked to the onset of lung cancer. The American

Cancer Society agrees and reports that a moderate smoker is ten times more likely to develop lung cancer than a nonsmoker. The good news is that when smoking ceases, the lungs, except in extreme cases, begin repairing themselves quite quickly. According to the American Cancer Society's pamphlet, "The Fifty Most Asked Questions," if a smoker stops before the onset of irreversible damage and does not resume smoking, after 10 to 15 years the ex-smoker's chances for disease are the same as those of someone who has never smoked, all other factors being equal. In other words, once you quit, the tar begins leaving your body quickly. Via this quick evacuation and the body's natural healing process, you should be breathing more easily and, all in all, be feeling healthier.

Carbon monoxide is not much better. Like tar, it is not seen as addictive. But again like tar, it is poisonous. When it is inhaled, it travels rapidly through the entire body.

It has the greatest impact on the red blood cells. Red blood cells distribute oxygen to the body's vital tissues. They are especially busy taking this oxygen to the heart. The inhaled carbon monoxide displaces this oxygen in these important cells, so their work becomes stifled. To compensate for the lack of oxygen to the heart and other tissues, the heart must beat faster and work harder, which it is already doing due to the intake of nicotine, discussed next.

In addition, smokers often acquire atherosclerosis, in which cholesterol-laden deposits clog the arteries in the heart and other parts of the body. According to the American Cancer Society, carbon monoxide can also impair vision and reduce attentiveness. As the heart is working harder, it needs more oxygen to work efficiently, but instead it's getting less oxygen.

Fortunately, we have fabulous bodies. When smoking ceases, the oxygen does restore itself. Our red blood cells begin traveling again, and our bodies begin rejuvenating.

Now comes the really rough one: nicotine. According to the American Cancer Society, nicotine from an inhaled cigarette reaches the brain in seven seconds. A smoker who smokes a pack a day inhales this drug, as well as others, approximately seventy thousand times a year! When nicotine reaches the brain, it immediately acts as a stimulant to the central nervous system. The American Cancer Society reports that nicotine causes blood pressure to rise and increases the heart rate by as many as 33 beats per minute. Nicotine is one of the most dangerous drugs in a cigarette. Sixty milligrams (about three drops) taken straight will kill a human being by paralyzing his or her breathing capacity. It is about as lethal as cyanide. The reason it does not kill the smoker is that it is taken in small doses, quickly metabolized, and excreted.

Nicotine is physically addictive. When you inhale, it travels directly to the brain and central nervous system. It speeds everything up, though later, depending on the dosage, nicotine can also act as a depressant. After repeated smoking, your body begins to "need" nicotine. When the level of the drug in your body starts to decline, your body senses the change. You then crave a "nicotine fix." When you light up, you almost immediately return your nervous system to its former state. This causes that familiar temporary relief. The feeling of "Gee, I needed that" is a common one. Unfortunately, for a heavy smoker, the relief lasts only about 20 to 30 minutes. That's why so many smokers feel the need for a cigarette every half-hour.

Brands with low tar and nicotine aren't much better.

According to the American Cancer Society, every puff contains chemicals like formaldehyde, lead, and ammonia, as well as carbon monoxide and some substances added for flavor and bulk, whose effects no one is yet sure of. Also, the smoker tends to inhale more deeply and smoke more cigarettes to compensate for the lower tar and nicotine. So cigarettes lower in tar and nicotine certainly are not safe.

Many smokers have heard about the stimulating effects of nicotine, yet don't believe these affects really exist. "I don't see how smoking can be a stimulant," they say, "because I feel so relaxed when I smoke." Or, "When I feel tense, the first thing I think about is a smoke. I immediately feel calmer." That relaxed feeling is caused by the nicotine refeeding the body. When the drug is almost diminished in your bloodstream, your body feels the effects immediately. As you inhale and your body stabilizes, there is an immediate feeling of calm. Also, for many people, the entire procedure of lighting up, playing with the cigarette, and so on has a calming effect. So actually, the feeling of relaxation is your body stabilizing itself into an unstable condition! That is, your body is working harder than it should in order to compensate for all the unnatural chemicals it has to metabolize.

Nicotine also causes the metabolism to speed up. Again, the body is working much harder, so more energy is expended. But the amount that the metabolism is speeded up due to nicotine intake is *not significant*. Therefore, as an ex-smoker's metabolism slows down and returns to normal, the change in metabolic rate is also *not significant*. The ALA says one-third of the people who quit gain weight, one-third stay the same, and one-third lose weight. Most research suggests that if all other factors, such as eating habits and health, remain the same, an ex-smoker's weight will probably not fluctuate more than five to eight pounds upon quitting. This weight fluctuation, if it does occur, will happen gradually within four to six weeks, provided the ex-smoker does not increase his or her caloric intake by a significant amount.

This means that, if after quitting, you go to town and eat everything in sight, you will gain weight. But be honest. The gain will not be due to metabolic change. A person who has quit smoking and gained 30 or 40 pounds has not gained weight because of a drastic metabolic change. If smoking were that powerful of a stimulant, there wouldn't be any overweight smokers. Major weight gain after quitting is rarely caused by metabolic change. It is from eating, and eating a lot.

Although nicotine is addictive, it can be flushed out of the body quite quickly. The American Lung Association says that when you quit smoking, nicotine is able to leave your body within a single week. To ensure that this process is quick and easy, drink lots of liquids, especially fruit juice (see Chapter 9). According to research done by Dr. Stanley Shacter of Columbia University, fruit juices, along with raw vegetables, help produce a more alkaline urine, thereby making the withdrawal process a little easier and more stable. In other words, the nicotine exits the body slowly, leaving you on a more even keel. This should also help make the nicotine cravings less intense. The physical need for the drug leaves within about seven days, and any urges after that are due to your emotional and social relationship with the cigarette.

One last word about nicotine. Many people who quit smoking complain about intense cravings for sweets. Studies have indicated that these extreme urges are partially due to heightened senses of taste and smell, as well as the emotional need to have something in one's mouth. But some current information has been offered by Dr. Neil E. Grunberg of the Uniformed Services University of the Health Sciences in Bethesda, Maryland. Dr. Grunberg suggests that nicotine may stimulate a change in the natural glucose available in the body. This means that smoking may lessen your natural appetite for sweets, and upon quitting, your natural glucose levels kick in and may increase your desire for sugars. The good news is that once your body readjusts its blood sugar level, this extra physiological desire for sweets does diminish. But it certainly would not hurt to see your doctor and have your glucose levels checked. The more you know about the physical changes your body is experiencing, the easier it will be for you to cope with your mood swings.

Since tar, carbon dioxide, and nicotine cause such important changes to the body, it's no surprise that giving up smoking produces a variety of symptoms. Being aware of them will help you feel confident so that you can stick to your new healthy way of eating and living. The following symptoms can be somewhat uncomfortable, but remember, if you experience any of them, they should last only about a week, and most of them are really quite tolerable. Fortunately some people never get any symptoms.

- Increased coughing: If you start coughing more, it is probably because now that your lungs are no longer being polluted, they are working diligently to clean themselves out. It's not easy getting rid of all that tar that has been building up over the years. Coughing usually lasts only a few days and can be remedied by taking cough drops or some mild cough medicine. Of course, if it persists, contact your physician.

- Constipation: One of nicotine's effects is to stimulate your large bowel. So when you quit, you are giving up one of the things that keeps you regular. If you find yourself becoming constipated, drink lots of water, eat some prunes, and have raisin bran for breakfast. (Of course, there is always good old castor oil!) If nothing seems to help, contact your doctor, but try to be patient. This, too, will last only a short while.

- Dizziness: This is usually due to your body getting more oxygen than it has been accustomed to. You need to give your brain a chance to refeed itself after having been starved for so long. Take slow, deep breaths and try to avoid alcohol—especially the first week. Alcohol cuts down the amount of oxygen your blood sends to your brain, so be sure to watch your alcohol consumption.

- Slightly sore and raspy throat: In addition to irritating your throat, tobacco numbs it. When you quit, the numbness begins to go away, and you'll begin to feel the irritation more acutely. To alleviate most of this discomfort, drink lots of cold fruit juices and suck on hard candies. Remember, it lasts only a short while.

- Nervousness and anxiety: Experts are still uncertain about how much nervousness and anxiety are due to physiological changes and how much they are due to the mental anguish of quitting. To combat the nicotine's effects, drink fruit juices and other liquids. Try to stay away from beverages containing caffeine.

- Trouble sleeping or sleeplessness: Along with nervousness and anxiousness, you may experience insomnia. Usually you can alleviate this condition with some deep breathing and relaxation exercises (see Chapter 9), as well as drinking warm milk before bed. Try to have a familiar and consistent routine before bedtime. For example: watch the news, wash your face, drink your milk, watch 15 minutes of Johnny Carson, read for 10 minutes, turn out the light, then say your prayers. Try to make it the same every night. If your insomnia persists longer than a week, consult your doctor.

- Lethargy: This is due to lack of sleep combined with the amount of mental energy it takes to stay away from cigarettes and the physical changes your body is going through. Your system is trying to regulate and normalize itself, which causes you to expend more energy than when you were smoking. You can usually get over this by doing some physical activity (see Chapter 9) balanced with plenty of rest and pampering.

In addition to the aforementioned uncomfortable physical symptoms, you may well experience some of these positive ones:

- Increased sex drive: Smokers often experience diminished sex drive. Once you quit, your sex drive returns. So enjoy!
- Increased stamina and energy level: Your ability to do physical activities is greatly increased. One smoker who loved to dance found that, upon quitting, she was able to boogie for over an hour straight, a feat her feet—and the rest of her—could never have accomplished while smoking.
- Much easier breathing
- For women: Increased chance for healthier pregnancies, decreased chance of bone loss (osteoporosis), and lack of facial hair. The Medical College of Wisconsin has discovered that women who smoke were 50 percent more likely to have facial hair than nonsmokers. This was apparently due to the effect smoking may

have on the ovaries, hormone metabolism, or both. So, for increasing the odds for beautiful skin, healthy babies, and strong bones, women should stay away from cigarettes.

- Normalized heart rate and blood pressure
- Whiter teeth
- Better smelling body, clothes, hair, and breath
- Improved sense of taste. (Debate rages on whether this is a positive or a negative.)
- Improved sense of smell: Now you can really smell the flowers!
- Fewer sore throats and colds: Ex-smokers often report that they are less susceptible to these minor illnesses. While you were smoking, airways narrowed and the natural immune system in your lungs was altered, so you were more likely to acquire colds, pneumonia, bronchitis, and emphysema. Quitting smoking gives you a chance to overcome those problems.

The good news for ex-smokers is the pattern these symptoms follow. The uncomfortable symptoms last only about one week. They do not appear in everyone, and when they do, they usually peak around the third or fourth day and then wane. After that, it's all down hill. Even better, the positive symptoms continue forever. Any uncomfortable symptoms that persist after the first week are considered to have a psychological origin. But don't fret—that's what the next few chapters will help you address.

# 3
# Smoking and Overeating: Habitual or Emotional?

Now that you know that most of the physical symptoms of quitting last only about one week, you have a basis for understanding the habitual and emotional attachment to smoking and overeating. One ex-smoker, Sandy, explained it quite well:

"I knew I had to quit. I was really getting scared. I would wake up in the morning and feel a heaviness in my chest. Breathing became more and more difficult. My kids were even beginning to cough when they were near me.

"So six months ago I did it! The first day was the most difficult. I felt spacey, as if I did not know what to do with myself. This spaciness was really the only major symptom I noticed. Sleep was no problem, my mood was OK, and almost immediately I felt as if I could *breathe*. The worst thing about the very beginning was feeling I needed something in my mouth and something to do with my hands. I tried sugarless hard candies and suckers as well as chewing on straws and toothpicks. But nothing felt right.

"Now things are much better. There are times I still find I have the urge for a cigarette, but those are usually the more stressful periods of my day. Some days I don't even think about it at all. I will say this, there is something familiar and therefore comforting about the entire action of smoking, and it is very difficult to find anything else to replace it. Meanwhile, as I stay away from smoking and even have come to the point where I find others who smoke offensive (the odor is such a turn-off), I find myself eating. I know I have been using food instead of cigarettes, and that too is bad for me. Though I do not want to die of cancer, I also do not want to live and look like a porker!"

As a therapist, I gave Sandy a lot of credit. She had already been astute enough to realize what was going on inside her. She knew she was substituting food for smoking. However, she seemed quite prepared and willing, if need be, to experience a little discomfort to redeem the long-term positives of quitting. Yet, when it came to exactly how much discomfort she was willing to tolerate, weight gain was where she wanted to draw the line. Her advantage was that she was not kidding herself that her weight gain was due to metabolic imbalance. She knew that those extra pounds came from extra eating. As we began working together and she gained understanding of the dynamics of her attachment to cigarettes and now food, she started the process of change—and weight loss.

Like many ex-smokers who come for therapy, Sandy is astute. Yet she and the others feel unable to free themselves from this relationship to cigarettes and, later, food. They just don't understand how to rid themselves of the addiction and get on with their busy lives.

In my therapy sessions, I begin by explaining what

this attachment is really about and why it is so difficult
to break. Most people start smoking in response to peer
pressure. Their friends are smoking, so they want to
belong, be cool, and feel as if they look more grown up.
But before long, they start enjoying it. The cigarette
becomes their friend, an extension of themselves, a
helper to make many situations, especially social ones,
run more smoothly. (Later you will see how food does
the same thing.) But in time, most heavy smokers
smoke just because it's a habit. They do it almost automatically without much thought or reason.

As mentioned in the Introduction, a person who
smokes a pack a day takes seventy thousand puffs in
one year. That's a lot of times for the hand to go back
and forth to the mouth! In and of itself, that behavior is
a difficult habit to let go of. In addition, the smoker
begins to associate the cigarette with many different
activities, such as talking on the phone, having a cup of
coffee, finishing a meal, watching television, starting
the car, playing cards, reading, and sitting at his or her
desk. As soon as these activities begin, the smoker's
automatic response is to take the cigarette out of the
package, twirl it in his or her fingers, maybe tap it on
the table, reach for a match or lighter, light up, puff
away, and then squish it in the ashtray. That is a lot of
activity that soon becomes rather comfortable and quite
rewarding. Like Pavlov's dogs, who learned to salivate
at the sound of a bell even when food was not present,
the smoker learns to "need" or desire a cigarette with
certain triggering situations.

I've found that most adults rarely begin smoking if
they've never smoked before. Most know that smoking
is unhealthy and few need the reassurance that they're
"cool" from middle-aged peers. Most of the time, smoking is an extreme turn-off to nonsmokers. However,

many ex-smokers who've quit for years return to the habit again when triggered by a particular stress.

From here on in, the majority of this book addresses the emotional aspects of the urge to smoke, and then the urge to overeat. It's important for you to try to begin discerning how many of your urges for a smoke or food are due to simple automatic triggers (stimuli) and how many are due to uncomfortable feelings. (See Chapter 4 for a list of specific ways to deal with typical automatic triggers.) Although you may often feel like having a cigarette or a snack due to a triggering stimuli, you probably grab for your "friendly fix" even more often because of the emotional comfort it elicits.

Smoking and/or eating are much more than just bad habits. When you do either activity to excess, you are probably using it as a comfortable elixir to drown feelings you'd like to suppress. Smoking and/or eating, even thoughts of them, serve as a powerful distraction from thoughts and feelings you don't like.

At a very young age, we all learn that food has loads of properties that have little to do with nourishment. Food is used for reward, punishment, fun, and comfort. I hate to admit this, but I have been known to offer one of my sons a cookie when he has brought home a sore knee. I have also been known to offer my kids ice cream as a reward if they would stop whining. And you know what? It works! So it's really no wonder that food provides a comforting alternative for the ex-smoker.

Food, weight, and smoking are effective distractors from whatever may be bothering us. Marital discord, job problems, too little money, parents, in-laws, children, friendships, sickness, and loneliness may all be factors that bring about the addictive behavior. Food, weight, diet, and smoking are certainly much easier to address, because they are more tangible. They are also more socially acceptable as problems. In other words, it is simpler to call a friend and complain about how hard it is to quit smoking and how your new diet isn't working than to disclose that you're feeling lonely and inadequate or are contemplating divorce.

So many people find in smoking or eating a powerful "friend" for combating stress, uncomfortable feelings, and any other yucky stuff. For as fortunate as human beings are to feel joy, love, passion, security, and fulfillment, it is also our fate to experience a varying amount of disconcerting feelings. While it is hardly the highlight of anyone's day to feel anger, sorrow, hurt, rejection, or guilt, rare is the person who can go through 24 hours without experiencing some of these uncomfortable states.

Though these feelings aren't pleasant, the degree of discomfort is usually exaggerated. This is due to our attitudes about these feelings. Instead of accepting them as part and parcel of the human condition and dealing with them as such, we label them as horrible and unacceptable. In order to combat ever having them, we tell ourselves we just *won't* have them. Now this is a problem, because have them we do!

For many of us, this avoidance process is quite intricate. As soon as we feel any of these feelings emerge, we quickly begin the denying process. We do this by lighting up or going to the refrigerator, smoking or eating with great intensity and commitment. And more often than not, those unpleasant feelings begin to fade.

People don't generally do this on a conscious level. No one I have ever worked with has said, "Oh, gee, I know I have lots of things I should be acknowledging, but since I don't want to, I think I will become a chain smoker or a compulsive eater." This attachment to the cigarette, and later to food, is, for the most part, unintentional. It evolves and turns into a standard manner of coping.

As children, we learn that we have lots of feelings. As we grow, we find different ways of coping with these feelings. Some kids withdraw into themselves, some watch television, some play with toys, some act out, and so on. But eventually, most of us figure out appropriate ways of dealing with life's frustrations.

A lot of lessons we learn and coping methods we choose are based on the messages we receive from our parents. At a very young age, we learn what kinds of feelings are acceptable and in what ways we are allowed to express them. These are what I call the family "rules." It's not that most parents stand up with a chart and say: "OK, children, on the left is a list of acceptable feelings and ways to express them, and to the right is the list of feelings you are not supposed to have and we find unacceptable to express." But somehow, we do get the message. It is precisely those feelings that you were "told" were unacceptable to have, let alone express, that today cause the most urges for a cigarette and, later, for food.

What kinds of feelings are these? For each person, the answer is different, but the generic answer is any feelings that were considered taboo in your household, any feelings that you still feel you should not have. Whether these feelings be anger, frustration, hurt, whatever, if you tell yourself you are not supposed to experience them, do not be surprised if after one of these feelings tries to surface, you start noticing a rather large desire for a smoke or a big snack.

For example, Mary is a homemaker and an ex-smoker who finds herself using food a lot more than she sees necessary. She has three children, ages six, eight, and ten. She would like to get out and find something more to do, especially since all her kids are in school full-time, but she isn't exactly sure what she wants. One of her closest friends, Laura, is also a mother. She has two kids, ages seven and nine. Three years ago Laura started her own business doing consulting work for large companies.

Mary looks forward to a monthly lunch date with Laura. However, Mary has begin to notice that every time they have lunch, Laura is a good 45 minutes late, arrives in a rush without voicing an apology, and then proceeds to chat incessantly about her work. Discussion of Mary's life is not a part of the afternoon's agenda. Each time they have lunch, Mary has noticed a tremendous desire for the entire basket of rolls.

Why are the rolls so important of late? One roll is tasty, but by the time you have eaten your fifth, taste and hunger is no longer relevant. Mary was probably experiencing some feelings she didn't like. Two of these feelings were likely anger and hurt—they usually go hand in hand. Mary was angry at her friend because Laura was continually late, and she was hurt because Laura showed no interest in her world. In addition, Mary was also probably feeling somewhat jealous of her friend's exciting work and a little depressed that her life seemed so empty. These latter feelings—especially the jealousy and inadequacy—were probably the toughest for Mary to acknowledge and accept. After all, a "true" friend should be happy for Laura and her success and any ambivalent feelings should be absent.

Many people do believe that the rules of friendship, motherhood, and business are all absolute. This view leaves little room for being human. The more Mary experienced what she labeled as "wrong" feelings and the more anxious she became, the more the rolls started to look good. If Mary had still been a smoker, she no doubt would have inhaled a great many cigarettes. Another person who coped with uncomfortable feelings by eating was Barbara, an enthusiastic 52-year-old. She had three grown children, worked two days a week with her husband, took a computer class one night a week, played bridge, and met friends for lunch. She quit smoking 10 months before I saw her. Her reasons for quitting were varied. She had been smoking for 20 years, so she knew her health was being affected. Her family and friends had kept bugging her and reminding her how unhealthy and offensive her habit was. She also had some private reasons, probably one in particular that broke the camel's back, that helped her make her last cigarette be just that—the last. (She did not feel like sharing her private reason, but that is not uncommon. If it made her quit, hurrah!) One of the reasons it took her so long to quit was the common fear of weight gain. Barbara was already overweight and scared to death she would gain a lot more.

We spent about a half-hour discussing what the most difficult times were for her, and how she dealt with her smoking and eating urges. She told me that the first two or three days had been the hardest—she had been crabby and vulnerable. If anyone looked at her cross-eyed, she would cry. After those initial days, she reported that she felt better and that for the first two weeks, there was not much difference in her eating. But over the next three months, she noticed a dramatic increase in her desire for snacks. She'd eat anything to have something in her mouth. Her savior was sugarless chewing gum. She chewed packs of it. She also admitted to indulging in lots of other things that were a bit more fattening.

She did not feel ready to diet. But she knew my approach was different, so she thought she would come in and hear what I had to say. After the first half-hour, I began explaining that in many cases the urge for a cigarette, and then for food after quitting, was really due to suppressed feelings. I explained how these feelings were uncomfortable and difficult to accept and how often people are frightened of these feelings and try to run from them. I went on to tell her that no matter how much we try to avoid these feelings, our inner voice will eventually catch up with us and force us to stop and listen. We discussed feelings about work, marriage, and family, as well as a variety of other things.

As I continued, Barbara began rummaging through her purse for a piece of gum. I stopped and asked her what she was feeling. "Nothing," she replied, "I just wanted a piece of gum." As we began exploring her sudden desire for gum, she became aware of uncomfortable feelings. I emphasized that our sessions would not be on what she should or should not eat, but how she was or was not dealing with her feelings.

Barbara, like most people, intellectually acknowledged that having uncomfortable feelings is part of being human. However, deep down, people like Barbara remain unconvinced. They've been raised to feel that these "awful" feelings are "wrong," and that people who feel them are weak. These rules hold especially true concerning our feelings for those we love. But to think we are never supposed to feel anger or hurt toward those we love seems a bit unrealistic. Feelings are not right or wrong—they just are. When we judge our own feelings, the urge to smoke or eat is usually close behind.

In order to define the feelings you are suppressing, look back on the behaviors that were considered taboo in your family when you were a child. For example, you might have come from a family of yellers and screamers. Your parents might have loved a good fight. But if anyone in that family came home with a problem that included hurt feelings, he or she might have received the message that exhibiting angry feelings is acceptable, but not expressing hurt ones. If you were feeling hurt, you probably would have been reprimanded for feeling sorry for yourself, reminded of all the people who *really* have it bad, and sent to your room. These are the kind of strong messages a child hears: I hurt, but I shouldn't.

Feelings are funny. We may try large doses of rationalizations and self-deceptions to keep the unacceptable feelings from surfacing. We may be adept enough to succeed at keeping them out of our consciousness enough to be productive. But these feelings need to be addressed. Usually, they are suppressed but emerge via an urge to smoke and, upon quitting, to eat.

Most of us soon discover that the pleasure of food, like the cigarette, lasts only a very short time, maybe 15 minutes to a half-hour. Then, not only does whatever we were suppressing still remain, but we feel horrible for stuffing our faces! So we promise ourselves we will be "good" tomorrow. (This being "good on my diet" is a catch phrase I have heard a thousand times.) Unfortunately, most of these promises are in vain.

We don't break our diets or start smoking again because we are weak, or stupid, or lack willpower. Good intentions fall to the wayside because they are directed toward the symptom (smoking or eating/dieting) rather than the cause. As long as this attention is misdirected, the attachment to smoking and then eating will take a long time to break. This is because feelings never go away. Each day they return and, if not dealt with directly, will eat at us until we eat them! Compulsive eating, as did smoking, gives us that short-term comfort we desire. It also gives us long-term misery.

As you can see, the relationship you develop with food

after you quit smoking is not really about food or about cigarettes. It's about how you are dealing with your life. You are not a crazy person who will never recover. Your eating urge, this desire for food, does have a cause: each time you have an all-encompassing urge to put something in your mouth, even though you know you are not physically hungry, there has probably been some precipitating situation, incident, or thought that left you feeling uncomfortable. This feeling was one you have been taught you are not supposed to feel. You judge the feeling and therefore yourself. To run from this feeling, you go directly, now that you have quit smoking, to food. Here is how it looks.:

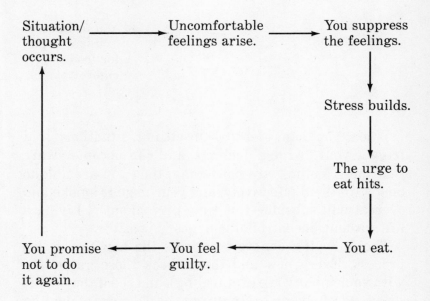

The entire process is cyclical and repetitive. No one can take away all your uncomfortable situations, thoughts, or feelings. The trick is to intervene with healthy alternatives before you reach a stress level that causes you to carry out the unhealthy alternative. A healthier alternative to the preceding cycle would go more like this:

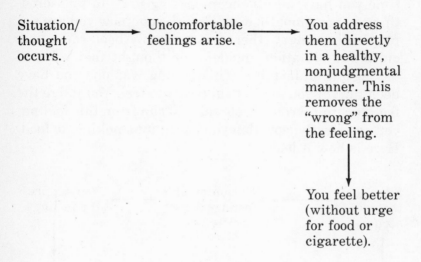

Situation/thought occurs. ⟶ Uncomfortable feelings arise. ⟶ You address them directly in a healthy, nonjudgmental manner. This removes the "wrong" from the feeling.

You feel better (without urge for food or cigarette).

When you can identify unsettling situations that trigger your "wrong" feelings, and can become aware that these feelings are not wrong, then you are able to deal with them effectively, and your urge to smoke and overeat will subside—this time permanently! Living a life without uncontrollable urges is possible.

The following chapters address the how-tos of this process. Every now and then, check those guidelines with your inner voice (gut feeling), and see if they make sense. As you begin to stamp out the old ways of dealing with your feelings and try new ones, the urges for a cigarette and food will be sent on their way. This is not a trick or a gimmick. It's really about curing the problem and not just the symptom. The realization that you can replace emotional desires for cigarettes and food with the desires for change and self-care is an important step to a life free of bad habits and an increase in self-control. In turn, having a life filled with self-care enables you to be able to follow a healthy "eating" plan such as the one offered in Chapter 9. Not only can you follow it, but you can do so without feelings of denial and deprivation.

# 4
# Step 1:
# Recognizing Your
# Triggers

By now, you may already have begun a bit of introspection. You may be looking at what types of triggering situations you are vulnerable to or what thoughts and feelings you consider "wrong" to express. These would be the feelings that now contribute to your multitude of urges for a cigarette or food at seemingly unusual times. That look is a good beginning, but you need to do more than look; you need to plunge in and really explore. The resulting awareness is the beginning step in diminishing unwanted urges for cigarettes and food.

## HABITUAL TRIGGERS

To discover what your own issues may be, start by considering typical "habitual" situations that often accompany the urge for a smoke and, later, food. This will help you be clear on knowing the source of your urges, whether they are due to common stimuli or emotional issues you wish to avoid. The table on the next page shows common smoking triggers. Next to each one is a suggested new way to cope. The key word here is *cope*. The suggested techniques will ease the desire for a cigarette and/or food. These coping techniques are short-term helpers that have been compiled from clients, interviews, and information from the American Lung Association and the American Cancer Society. This list is by no means complete. Feel free to come up with situations and solutions of your own.

# EMOTIONAL TRIGGERS

Besides these habitual triggers, we're subject to emotional triggers. These emotional stimuli are less cut and dried than the habitual triggers, so uncovering them takes a bit more attention. For help, keep a feeling diary. The feeling diary is essential because it will help you pinpoint your inner feelings while helping you develop behavior techniques to handle your urges. Keeping a diary will encourage you to face and resolve your personal emotional issues.

The endless battle you fight with yourself over not giving in to your emotional desires for a smoke or a snack takes a great deal of time and effort. This effort keeps you from dealing with other things in your life that might be more uncomfortable. Worrying about quitting or about weight gain keeps one's mind quite occupied. Many times I have asked those who come to me for help, "If I said, 'Abracadabra, you never have to worry about food, diet, your weight, or smoking,' what would you spend your time thinking about?" Most have no answer. Keeping this journal will help you come to terms with what you may be avoiding by staying "food involved."

Consider this scenario to illustrate how obsessively

| Habitual Triggers | New Coping Techniques |
| --- | --- |
| Having a cup of coffee | Read the paper (skip the coffee) |
| After a meal | Leave the table quickly/Walk/Brush teeth or use mouthwash/Chew sugarless gum |
| Starting the car | Chew sugarless gum or hard candy/ Squeeze rubber ball or hand exerciser |
| Watching TV | Knit/Crochet/Build models/Do jigsaw puzzles/Stretch/Solve crossword puzzles/Play solitaire/ Take deep breaths |
| Talking on the phone | Put phone in left hand (right if a lefty)/Doodle/Play with a paper clip/ File nails/If you wear glasses, polish them |
| Waking up | Wash face/Take shower/Have glass of orange juice/Eat a good breakfast/ Use mouthwash |
| Sitting at your desk | Play with paper clip/Doodle/Suck on toothpick or straw/Have sugarless candies on desk/Polish those eyeglasses |
| Washing dishes | Talk on the phone/Chew raw vegetables or low-calorie candy |
| Reading | Polish nails first and then let dry/ Read in bed/Take 10 deep breaths |
| Being at a restaurant | Sit in no-smoking section/Concentrate on conversation/Make a list of topics before you leave/Get up from table/Bring toothbrush and brush teeth |
| Playing cards | Chew hard candies or toothpick/ Have some "good tricks" ready |
| Bowling | Be the scorekeeper/Drink caffeine-free diet pop/Chew ice cubes |

dieting while not addressing your emotional state can keep you dishonest with yourself:

Molly is an ex-smoker. Since she quit, she has put on 25 pounds. She is now on her eighth "diet," hoping this will be the one to take off those extra pounds. Her first thought each morning: "I just want to be 'good' today. I'm really going to work hard to stay on my 'diet.' "

Fade to Molly's kitchen. She has just finished her breakfast of dry toast and coffee. Her sons, who were late for school, have left in a rush. They've both left half of their French toast on their plates. Molly finds herself looking at the French toast. It stares back and starts beckoning to her: "Come eat me. You had such a small breakfast. Don't waste me, people are starving in Africa." She picks up a corner of the French toast and brings it toward her mouth. She's rationalizing: "A little bite won't hurt." She bites, but panic sets in, and she quickly dashes to the garbage disposal and throws the French toast out. She made it without cheating! Yeah!

Cut to later in the day. Molly is at work and has had a confrontation with her boss. She has just finished her lunch of three ounces of dry tuna and raw vegetables and is nursing her diet cola. She finds her mind drifting to the candy machine. She decides she will walk over and take a peek. She begins with the internal debate: "Should I or shouldn't I; *that* is the question!" She pushes herself away and again makes it without giving in.

Cut to Molly's home later that day at the dinner table. She and her husband are eating while the children argue about not wanting to eat their vegetables. No one is interested in how hard she worked to fix this healthy dinner. She finds her eyes roving toward the platter of chicken. The inner struggle begins. "I can't," she says. But, alas, she does. She starts with the chicken, promising this will be all, but continues from there to cookies, ice cream, and whatever else she can find.

Fade into Molly's bedroom. Molly is lying in bed. Filled with self-beratement and disappointment, she feels depressed and fat. Her entire review of the day revolves around what and how she ate. She feels horrible and promises that tomorrow will be a "good" day.

During Molly's entire day, not once did she ask herself how she was feeling. Staying food- and diet-oriented without paying attention to yourself, your work, your family, and your feelings is a process that will surely slow the quitting process.

To shift your focus, keeping a feeling diary is essential. Write about the time of day, where you are, who you are with, and anything else that might have happened to you in the past one to five hours (sometimes these urges are due to a delayed reaction) that left you feeling uncomfortable, unsettled, uneasy, or whatever. Try to push yourself to think about even the most unimportant of the day's events. No matter how minor or trivial they may sound, write them down.

Next, jot down what you are feeling as you are writing. If you are not sure, guess. Probably you are feeling an emotion you judge as one you shouldn't be experiencing. A helpful way to begin is to pretend a friend is telling you about your day. Most of us are better at seeing other's feelings. Whatever you come up with, write it down without editing. You will be looking for patterns of emotional triggers that push you into thinking about smoking and/or eating.

The final question you need to answer is how smoking or eating will help you deal with yourself (and others).

The pages in your diary should look like this:

Time: _____

Place: _____

Who am I with? _____

What happened or what did I think about in the last one

to five hours that left me feeling uncomfortable, un-

settled, uneasy, unanything? _____

_____

What am I feeling right now? _____

How will smoking/eating help me deal with myself (or others)? _____

The time to pull out your journal and write is when you have a strong urge for a cigarette or food. You will seldom need to write if this urge manifests itself around one of the previously mentioned habitual times. Write when you are experiencing an overwhelming urge that seems to come out of the blue and when you are sure true physical hunger is not a consideration.

Try to write at least twice daily, but the more times you write, the better. Some ex-smokers have told me that though cigarette urges have disappeared, they crave food 24 hours a day. Does this mean they must write all day long? Of course not. Pick the urges that are the most intense, the ones that make you really antsy.

It is important to write *before* the cigarette or food goes into your mouth. This is when your feelings are the most intense. Also, not every desire for something to eat needs to be evaluated. For example, if after lunch you think something sweet would be tasty, but then forget the urge after a moment, you needn't bother jotting it down. However, if after lunch you begin to contemplate eating five candy bars, you'd better get busy writing!

As soon as possible, purchase a small spiral notebook. You should be able to keep it in your briefcase, purse, or even a large pocket. Your entries will give you the insight into what is going on in your life. Many people may find that keeping a journal is burdensome. Nevertheless, it is an important task in order to keep food from becoming your new emotional outlet. Like anything in life, if you are willing to put some time and effort into it, you'll find the benefits rewarding. The payoff will not only include freedom from an emotional involvement with food, but it will also include inner peace. In addition to those two positives, you will find you have a body at your desired weight.

The diary will unlock your feelings. As the door opens, you'll learn how to deal with your life. Some people do have difficulty putting their feelings into words. If this should happen to you, don't despair. Do the best you can, and try to avoid getting hung up on whether or not you're using proper grammar. This is not a writing course! Few of us can come up with an enthralling and clear analysis of our feelings on the very first attempt. To help you, here are three examples from what might have been in Molly's diary, had she kept one:

Time: *8:00 a.m.*

Place: *Home*

Who am I with? *Alone*

What happened or what did I think about in the last one to five hours that left me feeling uncomfortable, unsettled, uneasy, or unanything? *The only thing I can think of is how I hate it when the kids are late and then they don't put their dishes in the sink. I feel like they think I am their maid! On the other hand, I often need to remind myself, they are just children. Maybe I expect too much.*

What am I feeling right now? *I am not sure. I know I want that French toast, and then I feel stupid for wanting it. It's cold and soggy! Maybe I'm mad at the kids and then guilty for being mad.*

How will eating this French toast help me deal with myself (or others)? *It won't, and I know that intellectually, but I still want it!*

Time: *2:00 p.m.*

Place: *Work*

Who am I with? *Co-workers*

What happened or what did I think about in the last one to five hours that left me feeling uncomfortable, unsettled, uneasy, or unanything? *My boss has really been irritating me. He talks to me like he thinks I'm from a foreign country! I know I need to discuss some things with him, but I don't want to.*

What am I feeling right now? *Like I want candy. I probably also feel bad that I don't have enough guts to stand up for myself.*

How will eating candy help me deal with myself (or others)? *Well, it will get my mind off work. Other than that, it won't do a thing, and I'll feel terrible.*

Time: *7:00 p.m.*

Place: *Home*

Who am I with? *Family*

What happened or what did I think about in the last one to five hours that left me feeling uncomfortable, unsettled, uneasy, or unanything? *The kids are fighting, which really gets on my nerves. I also feel like no one appreciates me.*

What am I feeling right now? *Like I am a wimp! Why can't I stand up for me even at home? Meanwhile, the chicken is looking good!*

How will eating chicken help me deal with myself (and others)? *Make everything go away, at least for a while.*

As you can see, there's more to Molly's everyday life than sticking to her diet. Remember, the diary alone will not take away your daily stresses. But it will give you new insight to help you address your particular nuances. It will also give you new information to help you handle future stresses. Keeping this collection of situations, thoughts, and feelings will help you to avoid using food as a substitute for smoking. Freeing yourself from this emotional attachment to eating will make it a breeze to follow the *I-Quit-Smoking Diet* eating and activity plan.

Keep your diary for the next week. Each of your entries should not take longer than five minutes. If you want to write longer entries, that's fine, too. Do whatever makes you feel better. After your week is completed, read over your diary entries. Jot down what you notice about yourself. Then turn to the next chapter, where you will learn how to diagnose your own feelings.

# 5
# Step 2:
# Diagnosing Your
# Feelings

Now that you have kept your diary for a week, you're ready to look at what your entries mean. You've probably begun to notice new feelings as well as the certain times they are more significant. You should be starting to see a correlation between these significant feelings and when the overwhelming desire for food or smoking hits. Each time this urge manifests, flashers, sparklers, and blinkers should be going off in your head, screaming, "Stop! This is a feeling happening; don't eat it or smoke it!"

Analyzing your feelings is not always an easy process. You might notice you feel a little unsure or even a bit scared about what you are writing. Anytime we initially look at ourselves, it can be a bit scary. Most of us move slowly when attempting something new. Feeling uncertain is OK and perfectly normal. Keeping your thoughts and feelings in writing can be confrontational. When they are down on paper, there is no backing out.

The good news is that in the long run, you'll feel and look great. So keep going!

Diagnosing your feelings starts with analyzing situations and thoughts that are suspected of conjuring up "taboo" feelings. Since this book is entitled *The I-Quit-Smoking Diet*, it emphasizes how, after quitting smoking, one's relationship with food evolves as an emotional crutch. Keep in mind that you probably used cigarettes many times in a similar manner and at similar times. Since the purpose of this book is for you to be able, upon quitting cigarettes, to avoid gaining weight and even to lose a little, you need to see why food has so much appeal during emotionally trying times, and so throughout the rest of the book, we'll deal only with those food urges, and how to control them. This understanding, and ultimate detachment, will make following the eating and activity plans a snap.

The all-encompassing urge for food that seemingly comes from nowhere when we quit smoking is really due to judged feelings we suppress. These feelings fall into two groups: outward-vigorous and inward-vulnerable. This distinction should help you identify your feelings more quickly.

*Outward-vigorous* feelings are feelings we direct toward others (outward). They are often harsh (vigorous) in their nature. Feelings that fit this category are anger, jealousy, frustration, and intolerance.

*Inward-vulnerable* feelings are directed toward oneself (inward). They are usually softer in their nature (vulnerable). Some examples of these are hurt, sadness, loneliness, and inadequacy.

For every situation or thought that presents itself, we experience both sets of feelings. But one set is usually less acceptable to us than the other set. The less acceptable feelings are the set we judge as "wrong." Your job is to find out which set gives you the most difficulty. A person from the family of screamers probably has little trouble dealing with outward-vigorous feelings. These feelings are familiar and acceptable, and this person would probably place no negative judgment on these feelings when they surface. But a person who grew up in a family where inward-vulnerable feelings weren't acceptable to share would have a much more uncomfortable experience—as well as a large desire for french fries!

So look into yourself. If you think good people never get angry, then upon feeling annoyed, you might automatically judge yourself as bad. If you think anyone who cries is a baby, the next time you feel a tear in your eye, it probably will elicit a negative judgment. It is the set of emotions you feel the most uncomfortable acknowledging that is causing the food to look so appealing at the most unappealing moments. At these times, you are using food as comfort so you don't have to feel.

To help you see this even more clearly, consider the following scenario. This should give you some further insight into some of the "family rules" you were taught (but can change):

You are ten years old and in the fifth grade. On Tuesday you went to school, and your teacher was really on your back. She yelled at you unjustly, she made you clean the entire classroom, and she wouldn't even let you go to the bathroom. You left school furious. The following day, you returned. But this time it was your friends. They were not exactly being nice. They made fun of your new shoes, they picked you last for the kickball team, and you found out you were not invited to one of the kids' birthday parties. You left school ready to cry.

Which one of these experiences would you be most apt to share with your mother or father when you got home? Really think about it, and try to go by your first

gut reaction. If your answer is that you would have discussed the situation where you were angry but would
be hesitant to bring up the one where you were hurt,
you may still be living by those same rules: anger at
others is OK (outward-vigorous would be easy for you),
but feeling hurt and sad (inward-vulnerable) is not. If
you answered the opposite—you would have shared the
tearful situation but not the angry one—then you may
still be having trouble with harsher feelings (outward-
vigorous) and less difficulty dealing with softer ones
(inward-vulnerable).

Remember, even though intellectually you may agree
that all feelings are fine, if you have an unconscious
"should not feel" message, eating urges will abound.
Each time you judge or deny a feeling, watch out Bas-
kin-Robbins!

Here is an example of how suppressed feelings mani-
fest into eating urges. A mother of two small children,
ages two and five, quit smoking three years ago. She
came to me because she found herself always thinking
and worrying about food, diet, and her weight. At one
particular session, she told me her daughter had the
flu. The previous night, her younger child threw up
four times, which forced this poor women to change the
linens repeatedly through the night. Each time the
younger child awoke, the older one asked for that all too
common "last" drink of water. By the fourth episode,
the mother was ready to share several very loud words
with both the kids. She lost her patience and snapped at
her children to "Get in bed!" Alas, just as she thought
everyone was taken care of and she had returned to her
bed, her youngest child had one final episode. The
woman got up, did her motherly thing, and headed to
the kitchen to eat last night's leftovers.

What caused this urge for last night's leftovers? My

initial guess was frustration, but as she openly discussed her frustrated feelings, I didn't think they were the culprits. So I probed deeper. Which feelings had she experienced that she had judged as not OK? She was upset she had not handled the situation better, by not raising her voice, remaining calm, and caring.

This woman was falling short of some ideal she had set up for herself in her role as a mother. (We all know good mothers never yell!) Rather than acknowledging her anger for having to be up all night, she pushed the feelings away and ate. Denying feelings is a sure-fire way to guarantee an overwhelming urge to eat. In our sessions, we worked on shifting some of her unrealistic expectations as well as her judgments.

Another example might look like this:

It's 10:00 P.M., often a difficult time for those who are emotionally attached to food. Sam quit smoking a year ago. He used to smoke heavily in the evening, and he has since found himself turning to food. Sara, his wife, is aware of his new attachment and is not too pleased with it. On this particular evening, Sara is on the phone, and Sam is watching television. Sara stays on the phone for over two hours. Sam would like her to get off and spend some time with him. But he knows she worked all day and cooked dinner, so he feels, being a liberated and considerate guy, that she does deserve her free time. His thoughts go something like this: "I should understand and should not feel left out, bored, or uncared about." However, it's not long before he finds himself eating a large bowl of buttered popcorn. Rather than acknowledge and accept his softer, inward-vulnerable feelings, he suppresses them and turns to food.

It wasn't Sara's fault Sam went for food. Sam denied his feelings and "pretended" they did not exist. This denial and pretending, along with making harsh judgments, are what make food so appetizing during a variety of feelings.

For practice in reviewing entries in your feelings diary and diagnosing your feelings, try to diagnose an actual entry from one of my clients. We will call her Beth. Since she had quit smoking two years ago, Beth had gained some weight and had come to me for counseling. As you read her entries, see if you can figure out which category of feelings she has trouble dealing with. Read each section carefully, trying to read between the lines.

Time: *10:00 a.m.*

Place: *Home*

Who am I with? *Alone*

What happened or what did I think about in the last one to five hours that left me feeling uncomfortable, unsettled, uneasy, or unanything? *The kids are driving me crazy. I made their beds, and they unmade them. They were late for the bus, and I had to drive them to school. On the way home I wanted to stop at the bank, and there was tons of construction so I said forget it. When I walked in the door, the phone was ringing and it was my friend canceling our lunch date for the 10th time. She had a business appointment.*

What am I feeling right now? *Like I want to eat! It's only 10:00 in the morning. My whole day is empty. I want to eat lunch now! I hate having to worry about what I eat. I hate myself.*

How will eating help me deal with myself (or others)? *I really don't know. I just want it.*

Time: *2:30 p.m.*

Place: *Home*

Who am I with? *Alone*

What happened or what did I think about in the last one to five hours that left me feeling uncomfortable, unsettled, uneasy, or unanything? *Nothing I can think of. I have been eating all day long. Back and forth, snooping in the refrigerator. I am not even eating things I like, just eating. The children will be home soon. John called and said he would be home late. He's playing tennis. I hate when he's late. I don't know what I am supposed to do with myself for the rest of the day and night. I have so much, why can't I just be happy?*

What am I feeling right now? *Nervous and stuffed!*

How will eating help me deal with myself (or others)? *It doesn't so why do I keep doing it?*

What kinds of feelings do you think Beth does not want to admit feeling? Try to read between the lines and into what's really going on in her life.

Let's look at the first entry. Considering Beth's harsher feelings, she seems annoyed with the kids, but she seems willing to acknowledge these feelings. However, she seems hurt and upset that her friend canceled lunch, and these are the uncomfortable feelings she's suppressing.

The second entry suggests a similar pattern. Beth is able to acknowledge her displeasure at John's tennis date, but she's afraid to focus on her self-image and how she will take care of herself for the rest of the evening. Again, rather than addressing her feelings of emptiness, she pushes them away, telling herself she has no right to feel them. "I should be happy," she thinks and turns to the refrigerator.

As you analyze your own entries, search to uncover what types of feelings are difficult for you to admit owning. What types are easy? If you have trouble diagnosing your words, put the diary aside for a while and then pick it up and pretend you are reading a friend's journal. Hunt for those feelings, and find out how and where you keep them inside. See what kind of detective you can be.

Another point worth emphasizing is that both examples involve significant others. I think it would behoove you to examine how often key people in your life are present when you find yourself needing comfort for uncomfortable feelings. This is why the question in your diary asking "Who am I with?" is important. For example, if you notice every time your boss steps into the room, you find your mind drifting to thoughts of luscious sweets, I would determine you have some feelings about your boss that you want to avoid confronting. Or perhaps each time you visit your mom you notice you find yourself nibbling on anything and everything, knowing your mom is hardly Julia Child and has even been known to cook things for so long you aren't sure what they are! I would again deduce there are some unresolved issues between you and mom!

Before you begin your new week, here are two sample entries for you to evaluate. See if you can determine what's really going on (that is, which feelings this woman judges to be no-nos).

**Entry #1:**

Time: *3:00 p.m.*

Place: *Home*

Who am I with? *Family*

What happened or what did I think about in the last one to five hours that left me feeling uncomfortable, unsettled, uneasy, or unanything? *Well, there had been a huge rainstorm. I just went down to check our basement, and there was over a foot of water! All my computer stuff is down there. When I ran up to tell my husband, he seemed very unconcerned. His answer: "Not much we can do. We'll just have to do without. I guess you'd better bring your computer upstairs." I suppose he is right, even though his attitude infuriates me! There really isn't that much down there, and I have already heard on the radio that some people lost everything. I guess I should be grateful, but all I want right now are potato chips!*

What am I feeling right now?

Outward-Vigorous: _____

Inward-Vulnerable: _____

How will eating help me deal with myself (or others)? *Not much!*

**Entry #2:**

Time: *3:00 p.m.*

Place: *Office*

Who am I with? *Co-workers*

What happened or what did I think about in the last one

to five hours that left me feeling uncomfortable, unsettled, uneasy, or unanything? _Everything seems to
be going fine. I just completed a major project, and
my boss approved. He's not much for showering a
person with praise, but I know that's just him. I do
feel a little bad, but I know I really shouldn't feel
angry. All I know is that I want to finish all the
sweet rolls in the coffee room. Sometimes I think
going back to cigarettes is the answer._

What am I feeling right now?

Outward-Vigorous: _____

Inward-Vulnerable: _____

How will eating help me deal with myself (or others)?
_Got me!_ _____

After reading these entries, my analysis looked like
this:

*Entry #1:* Outward-Vigorous—anger and lots of it,
both at her husband and the flood; Inward-Vulnerable—hurt, sad, self-pity.

*Entry #2:* Outward-Vigorous—annoyed at boss's lack
of appreciation; Inward-Vulnerable—hurt for the same
reason.

Keep your journal for another week. Try to stay attuned to the insights you have made from reading this
chapter. With your awareness higher, you can take advantage of healthy alternatives to smoking and overeating.

# 6
# Step 3:
# Replacing Food with Healthier Alternatives

With your awareness of your feelings more astute, you're ready to discuss what you are going to do to deal with them more effectively, other than smoke or eat. For though awareness is good and becoming nonjudgmental is a step in the right direction, they're not enough. Finding and using healthy replacements for food is what usually takes you that extra step toward feeling great. Not that you will never feel uncomfortable again, but your tolerance and ability to deal with this discomfort will be less scary and therefore more manageable.

But do remember, eating and smoking are coping mechanisms that work for the moment. Neither one resolves long-term issues and feelings. This chapter offers other coping mechanisms. They too help you feel better for the moment, but they won't resolve your problems. So as you read the suggestions—and some may sound a bit off the cuff (though no more unusual than devouring an entire cake in one sitting!)—be willing to give them a whirl. If you incorporate them into your daily life, you should notice a drastic difference in your feelings about yourself, those around you, and food.

This chapter discusses a variety of feelings. For each feeling, I will suggest ways to ease some of the discomfort. Since every feeling state has a need, this is an important part. Once you know what your emotional needs are, then you can determine how to get them met, other than with food. As you go through this process of recognizing feelings, identifying needs, and satisfying needs, you will be on your way to emotionally detaching yourself from food, this time permanently.

I am going to begin with three feelings I have found to be the most common precipitators for the urge to overeat: anger, hurt, and boredom. As you will see, all feelings can be dealt with and eased without using unhealthy vices.

## ANGER

Let's begin with anger. Some people have a difficult time with anger. This difficulty is often due to ingrained beliefs about how "awful" it is to experience anger, let alone display it. These beliefs generally come from home and society. A well-bred, refined, polite, sophisticated lady or gentleman does not get angry. If on the rare occasion the unmentionable happens (anger surfaces), such a person works very hard not to exhibit it. Anger is so unthinkable that, rather than admit its existence, many people run to the pantry for relief. Ironically, this kind of eating is voracious, certainly not refined or polite. The biting, chewing, and chomping, all done in record-breaking time, are how anger is released.

Alas, anger is an inevitable reality. It's one of those emotions, like it or not, that every human has to experience. Anger is a basic human reaction to an experience that hampers us from achieving a goal. This goal can be anything. If you want to go from here to there and a truck is blocking the way, you will probably feel perturbed. If you want to date someone special and that person is not available, you will probably feel frustrated. If you want a new job and it's already taken, you will probably feel upset. Since most of us do not always get what we want when we want it, anger is going to pop up every now and then.

So what do we need when we feel angry? Well, one thing for sure, holding it in and eating has not been working! What we do need is to ventilate it, release it, *get it out!* A good way to do this venting, other than chowing down, is to *hit*. Don't get nervous; I am not supporting being abusive to others! Instead, purchase a small Wiffle bat, and when these feelings start to emerge, go into a separate room and hit your bed, your pillow, a punching bag, the floor, or whatever (as long as it's not breakable or living). If you don't want to buy a bat, you can use a towel and hit it against your bathroom tile. (This makes a really loud noise!) The point is to let your angry feelings out. Hitting your bed, pillow, punching bag, floor, title, or whatever does not hurt anyone else and does help you. You can also try yelling and screaming—behind closed doors of course, or in your car. Sound strange? *Yes!* Does it work? Definitely.

Why do hitting and the other alternatives I will be presenting help you deal directly with your feelings? First of all, when you give yourself permission to deal with your feelings directly, you begin to feel like you are gaining *control* of your emotions. When you can say to yourself, "I have anger and it's OK. Here is how I plan to deal with my feelings," you'll feel an overwhelming

sense of being in charge of yourself. So many of my
clients say they feel out of control when it comes to
"dieting." Their food intake is where they focus their
attention rather than their lives. Deciding to accept
yourself and the variety of feelings you will surely experience throughout life, and taking affirmative action in
how you will consistently react to these feelings, allows
you to deemphasize the entire "food" issue. Instead of
the emotions controlling you, you are now controlling
them. But don't misunderstand: controlling them
doesn't mean pushing them away. Quite the contrary!
You are controlling them by letting them surface and
choosing to deal with them on *your* terms, not theirs.

The second reason hitting and the other alternatives
work is that hitting allows you to feel the *intensity* of the
anger. Most people are afraid of experiencing their
feelings, especially the ones they have judged as wrong.
Hitting allows you to experience the feeling in a non-
threatening manner. Once experienced, the feeling is
no longer so threatening and therefore is less scary and
more manageable. The situations or thoughts that triggered the anger may not disappear, but the actual intensity of the feeling will.

The final reason hitting and the other alternatives
are important is that they tend to have a *triggering* effect. Once you begin hitting about one situation,
another troublesome situation or thought often surfaces. Remember, many people suppress and push
away these uncomfortable feelings. They are so hidden
that people don't even know they are there . . . until the
kitchen beckons! By hitting, you allow suppressed emotional issues, ones you didn't even know you were still
upset about, surface.

So no matter how ridiculous this behavior sounds,
please try it. You might feel a little foolish at the onset.

But you probably won't feel any more foolish than you have after eating too much.

There may be times that you discover you are angry when hitting is inappropriate. Obviously, if you are at a party, you cannot just excuse yourself and go in the other room and hit! But do not fear, other options are available for times where ventilating loudly is impossible. For example, you can leave the room and scream in your car, you can leave the room and write about whatever you are upset about, you can keep a hard rubber ball in your purse or jacket pocket and squeeze it, you can write a prolific letter directly to the person who upset you (though I wouldn't recommend mailing it), you can pull a friend aside and vent your feelings to him or her. The bottom line is that there is always something available to help you with your feelings beside the buffet table, the candy machine, the kitchen, or the nearest 7-Eleven! All of these alternatives are healthy ways to deal with anger. As does food, these outlets help you to feel better quickly. But unlike food, they have the added benefit of making you feel good about yourself.

You may be wondering about the option of expressing your feelings to the person who upset you. I haven't mentioned it because I don't recommend being direct with someone else until you can be direct and honest with yourself. When you are working hard at getting in touch with your own feelings, it is not always wise to share every newly discovered emotion with the entire world! You do not have to tell your local grocery clerk your innermost feelings. At this stage it's critical that the person who knows how you feel is *you.*

This is not the 1970s when we were taught assertiveness was the route to self-enhancement. Everyone, wanting to self-enhance, took this bit of advice to the extreme. Friends, relatives, neighbors, business associates, no one was safe! Fortunately, it didn't take most of us too long to realize if we continued on this path, we would have friends, relatives, neighbors, and business associates who didn't want to talk to us! There is nothing wrong with sharing your feelings with the significant people in your life at appropriate times. But for now, be cautious. Sharing a feeling at the wrong time in the wrong manner can leave you with an entirely new set of uncomfortable feelings—feelings that may lead you down the path to the kitchen.

# HURT

Moving on to another feeling that contributes to us staying attached to food, let's take a look at hurt. This is another one of those emotions most of us would prefer to do without. But like all feelings, it's one we're inevitably going to experience. When we are feeling hurt, we need the same thing a child needs when he or she is feeling hurt. We need some comfort. How do we give kids comfort? Usually a good old-fashioned hug. Well, that's what we need, too—a hug! If you think about it, a hug makes sense.

When children feel hurt, they innately know to go to parents for cuddling, but if Mommy and Daddy are not available, they run to their teddy bear. They talk to it, hold it, pet it, and shortly thereafter feel better. You can do the same thing. If a person is available for a hug, that's great. But often the person we want the hug from is the exact person who has hurt us! So go out and purchase (or borrow from your kids) a nice soft, cuddly teddy bear. When you notice you are feeling empty due to hurt, sadness, on a similar emotion, go into a private place, somewhere where it is nice and quiet, and hug your teddy bear. Tell your bear how sad and hurt you feel. Really get into it!

I know this sounds just as unusual as the hitting, but again, it's no more silly than devouring an entire bag of Cheetos! Will the hugging make whatever you're feeling hurt about disappear? No, but it will make you feel better . . . just as food has done. It will also contribute to your feeling more in control of your life. It will help you feel the intensity of your hurt so it will be more manageable next time, and it might trigger other feelings you didn't even know you were hiding.

For those times when you can't go into a private place and hold your teddy bear, there are other options. You can write about your sad feelings, or you can keep a tape recorder handy and talk to yourself about your feelings as though you were talking to a friend. You can call a friend and ask for some sympathy. Hugging or doing any of those other replacements will diminish your urges for food, enabling the emotional way you use food to lessen. I know this may be difficult to believe, but once you start taking care of your emotional needs directly, food—instead of being an outlet for your emotional states—becomes an enjoyable, delicious, and healthy part of your life. By allowing yourself to feel hurt, and by accepting and gratifying the need for comfort, you make food an unacceptable option for self-consolation.

# BOREDOM

Let's move on and discuss boredom. Before quitting smoking, many people found that the days when they were just hanging about with nothing to do were the days they bought extra packs of cigarettes. Since quitting, they notice that when they have those kind of days, or even hours, food is beckoning! Their comments go something like this: "Sometimes there is nothing to do. I hate just hanging around." Or: "Some days I have lots of things I could do, but I just don t feel like it. Those days are so boring." Rather than address these hours and themselves, they find they are being seduced by leftover meatloaf!

Boredom is not really a feeling. It's a state of being. When you have lots of time on your hands with nothing specific that you have to do or want to do, you are looking, at least on the surface, for something exciting, fun, interesting, or whatever to keep you busy. But it goes deeper than just lacking business. When we have nothing to do and are feeling bored, we tend to look into ourselves. Since there is nothing too interesting happening on the outside, we look within. Often, what we see does not meet with our approval. Questions start surfacing, questions such as: "Why is everything so boring? How come I have nothing to do? How come no one has called me to get together? How come I can't find anything to do to make me feel good? What's wrong with me? Why can't I just get it together?" Somewhere around these last three questions would be about the time food would start its seduction!

So what do we need, other than meatloaf, when boredom strikes? Having some fun options handy is usually a beginning. Activities that come to mind might be reading a good book, going on a bicycle ride, taking a walk, going to the library, renting a video, going to the movies, reading *People* magazine, ice-skating, rollerskating, cleaning your drawers and closets (I just love that feeling when my drawers and closet are clean!), making love, or anything else you might find stimulating. If you can't find anything that really grabs you, try to take the time available and just be with yourself. No judgments, no analyzing why you are not busy, just relaxing and being with you. Take this time and see what *you* really need.

# GUILT

After anger, hurt, and boredom, guilt is the next common emotion to elicit that all-encompassing urge for food. Guilt is a bit of a problem because of its nature. Unlike anger, hurt, and boredom, guilt is derived from inner value conflicts. It's usually about something we did or didn't do that we not only regret, but that makes us feel like we are a bad person. The causes of guilt for each of us are different. But when we feel it, many of us put a moral judgment on our entire personhood. When trying to figure out what we need when feeling guilty, the answer is more complex than hitting, hugging, or ice-skating.

With guilt the first thing you need to do is some serious introspection about who you are and what your values and priorities are all about. For example, when my mother became a parent, staying home with the children was seen as the appropriate "good" thing to do. So every day at lunch, she was there with a well-balanced meal and a hug and a kiss. Mothers who were not at home to give this nutritious and loving lunch were looked down upon, and some were even ostracized by other "decent" mothers. You'd better believe those mothers who had to work for financial reasons or, even worse, needed to work for their own mental health were racked with large doses of guilt! Today it is a bit different. If you "only" stay home with the kids and do not do things that are "productive," you are looked down upon. Even though people say it's OK to be home, the underlying feeling is they really don't mean it. Today, staying home all day can produce the same guilt that 30 years ago brought accolades! With guilt, then, it's not so much the actual circumstance or situation as it is our interpretation and belief system about the event.

The second thing you need to do with guilt is relabel

the word and concept. I like using the word *remorseful* instead of guilty. Remorse does not connote judgment about one's personality or character. It suggests uncomfortable feelings about a particular behavior. For example, if your mother-in-law calls you and you find yourself being short with her, you might feel bad about your behavior. But feeling bad about one's behavior rather than feeling you are a horrible person allows room for quick rectification. You can call and apologize to Mom, take her out to lunch, send her flowers, write her a sweet letter, and so on. On the other hand, if you label yourself as a terrible, unworthy soul, the methods to rectify your entire being would be much more difficult and abstract, and therefore harder to resolve. Using a judgmental way to deal with issues can make you feel helpless. Feeling this helplessness is not an uncommon time for turning to food.

After this relabeling, the third thing you need to do with guilt is to go ahead and deal with (resolve) the guilt-producing situation. For example, upon discovering through a mutual friend that you are driving into the city that day, a neighbor calls and asks you for a ride. You are going but had planned a lovely day with your husband. Saying no to your neighbor makes you feel awful. You can feel the guilt grinding inside of you.

What can you do? Stop and reevaluate why you feel horrible. Upon figuring that out (you know you always like to be liked), you decide to adjust your attention away from your personhood and onto the situation. It's not that you don't want to be obliging, but you also want to take care of you. So you call your neighbor back and explain the situation and offer her the following three alternatives: (1) You would be happy to check out the train schedule and drive her to the train; (2) You offer to rent her a limousine or a cab; (3) You ask if she would like to wait until next week, when you will go with her and make a day of it.

To summarize, dealing with guilt (remorse) is a three-step process. First, reevaluate your issues and check out those "should" statements. Then relabel the feelings. Finally, come up with a plan of action to resolve the situation at hand. This process will increase your odds of weight stabilization and even loss.

# TENSION

Another feeling that often causes folks to use food for comfort is tension. In today's world, we are all bombarded with so many outside stimuli, it's no wonder we feel stressed out and tense. If you are feeling tense, you need to feel relaxed. And what does relaxation look like to you? For each of us it is different. Eating is one option, but I would like to offer some healthier ones!

Things people have found to be helpful include taking a nice, hot bubble bath with lots of yummy soaps and soft sponges, getting a massage, reading a trashy novel, reading a classy novel, doing needlepoint, playing solitaire, talking on the phone, watching your favorite soap opera, writing a letter to a friend, reading *The National Enquirer*, doing your nails, and taking a nap. You can pick any of the above or choose your own. The main thing is to give yourself permission to do it and then go! Many people seem to feel "guilty" for taking time for themselves. They feel they don't deserve it or it is a waste. As we have already addressed guilt and have mentioned how important it is to take care of yourself, you can take some old rules and toss them!

An example comes to mind when I think of Sharon. Sharon had just been on vacation. She had a fabulous time. She relaxed and truly enjoyed herself. During the entire trip, food was not one iota an issue. She ate three normal meals a day and was fine. But as soon as she arrived home, forget it. The daily pressure was on, and so was the desire for sweets. Sharon felt she had to get everything done immediately: the laundry, the bank, getting the mail, the cleaners, the phone messages, and the grocery store. She felt everything had to be completed in one day or less.

As we discussed what her "unexplainable" eating was about, Sharon began to see that though fulfilling one's responsibilities is certainly an important part of life, so is taking time for ourselves. As much as work is an integral part of life, so should enjoyment and relaxation be. If you don't learn how to balance the two, even after a vacation, the cost is high . . . not only on the scale, but also in the tension generated around those you love. Through our talk, Sharon knew the answer was not to say "Hurrah, I have found my true inner self, so I never have to do anything for anyone else. My purpose here on earth is to pamper me for 24 hours a day!" If Sharon had done that, she would have felt horrible, too. But she did agree that in one's day-to-day life there has to be a balance of work and play.

Another way to help alleviate tension is to take a look at the stressful situation and try to reinterpret the events involved. I did a local cable show about three years ago. The topic was, ironically enough, stress. We had taped for several hours, only to find out there was something wrong with the sound. We had to redo the entire program. Talk about stress! My co-host and I stopped and tried to calm ourselves down. In the course of our discussion, we came up with a new format that we felt was going to work much more effectively than what we had just completed. The more we delved into our new plans, the more excited we became.

Sitting down and trying to work with and reinterpret

tense situations helps you come up with endless possibilities. Just knowing there are options available can turn tension into positive energy. So when tense, look for new ways of seeing the problems at hand, check out your options, give yourself some time for you, and you will not find yourself going to the refrigerator. Doing what you need to do releases tension in a positive and healthy way.

# FEELING TRAPPED

Another troublesome feeling is that of being trapped. There is nothing worse than feeling you are in a situation with no way out. This can be in a relationship, an unsatisfying job, difficult financial circumstances, or whatever. When we are feeling trapped, we generally need to feel freer. We need to feel less confined and more independent. We need to be able to see there are choices and options.

There are things (other than eating) that you can do to alleviate this feeling and achieve more of a sense of freedom. For example, say you feel trapped in your job. You hate it and feel unfulfilled, but right now you need the security of that weekly paycheck. To begin freeing yourself from this trapped sensation, you need to begin to look at how, under the given circumstances, you can start taking advantage of the perks of the job (every job, even a horrible one, has some advantage!). If your boss is not picky about the length of the lunch hours, take a few minutes longer and go for a nice walk, buy yourself some flowers for your desk, or go on interviews. If you have great health and dental insurance, make an appointment to get your teeth fixed. If there are some people at work you find interesting but you have not made a move to be more social, now may be the time to make after-work plans. You need to do something to make the situation a bit more tolerable. So making the commitment to yourself that each day you will take care of yourself the best you can, even under unpleasant conditions, can tremendously alter how you feel about yourself and the situation.

As with all our emotions, when feeling trapped, we need to consistently remind ourselves our feeling state is legitimate. You are allowed to feel the way you do at any time. It's what you do with these feelings that is important. If you really get stuck about what to do, don't forget to think about asking a friend for help. Brainstorming with a friend can be a highly productive experience as well as a lot of fun. Together you are bound to come up with some things you can do to feel more in charge of your life. The freer you feel, the less likely you are to emotionally abuse food.

## FEELING INADEQUATE

What about feelings of inadequacy? That's another one of those heavy emotions that is hard to lighten. All of us, no matter how self-confident we may be, at times feel inadequate. We may have felt we did something inefficient at work or felt we were insensitive to someone else's feelings. When these situations arise, unfortunately our means of handling them is to give ourselves an emotional thump on the head and proceed with our day internally abusing ourselves. Such self-talk might be: "I cannot believe I made that mistake on that report. I am so incompetent!" Or: "I forgot to call Mary yesterday, and I just know she's going to think I am terrible!" It's amazing how many people distort and exaggerate their imperfections. Most of the people I deal with are fabulous. I constantly find myself telling them that I only wish they felt about themselves the way I do!

Feelings of inadequacy often stem from childhood, so

it is hard to offer simple alternatives for dealing with these long-lasting issues. But that doesn't mean they can't be addressed without eating and with healthier options. When feelings of inadequacy start nagging, what you really need to do is stop and think. Is your interpretation of yourself based on reality? If you are not sure, call a friend and discuss it. If you have someone you trust and with whom you can openly share how you feel, that friend can give you an objective viewpoint and assist you in putting things more in perspective.

In addition to doing more rational self-talk and discussing your self-image with a friend, another helpful alternative is to do a role play. Take an empty chair. Sit across from it. Now tell the chair how inadequate you are. Really sell it! Then move over and sit in the chair. See if you buy what "you" are selling. In most cases you will find yourself comforting "you!" This comforting will take place quickly and directly. Upon completing the role play, you should find yourself feeling much better, and you won't even have needed to eat a roll!

The more you can accept that you are not perfect (and who is?), the more you can accept that on occasion we all feel self-doubt. Self-doubt is understandable and something to consider and evaluate as each situation comes up. But to continually label yourself as inadequate for everything is unrealistic and untruthful.

## FEELING UNATTRACTIVE

Another common feeling state that can bring on an eating episode is feeling unattractive. And what do we need when feeling unattractive? Certainly not a bag of potato chips! What we do need is to feel *more* attractive. If you wake up each morning and do not do your hair, put on your makeup or shave, and take a little care in what you wear, that is not exactly a surefire way to increase your odds of good feelings! Of course, dressing up every day won't solve all your problems. But we are total human beings, which means we do have an outer self to consider as well as an inner self. Though we all have been taught that it is who we are on the inside that really counts, it doesn't hurt to take time for the outside also. This is especially so if we are going to be honest and realize that we, like it or not, live in a society that is extremely visually oriented.

For example, I had a female client who upon each visit, though she always looked neat and clean, was very plain. She never wore any makeup, jewelry, or cologne. Now, if she was happy this way, great. I certainly am not suggesting every woman needs to wear makeup, jewelry, and cologne to feel attractive. You need to decide what feeling attractive looks like for *you*. Anyway, for my client this was an issue. She would come in and tell me how she hated to look in the mirror. When I asked if there was ever a time she felt she looked good, she answered in the affirmative. Whenever she went to a fancy occasion such as a wedding, and got dressed up and took the time to apply makeup, dig out her nice earrings, and spray on her favorite scent, she felt better. When I asked why she didn't do some of that each day, her answer went something like this: "I would feel so selfish and egotistical. Isn't putting on makeup, and all that, superficial?" The more we explored her feelings about taking time for herself, the more it was clear she felt she didn't deserve to feel and look her best.

I offered a different, less extreme way of looking at makeup, clothes, and her need to take care of herself. You don't have to spend hours each morning in front of the mirror. Who has time at 7:00 A.M. to do that? But that does not mean you can't find fifteen minutes. Her ideas about her self-care were so extreme that there was little room for her even to do some little things to make her feel better about herself without also feeling she was being superficial and egocentric. So I suggested to her, as I am to you, that spending a little extra time on your personal appearance, though not the be all and end all of problem solving, is self-nourishing. Much more nourishing than potato chips!

## FINDING THE RIGHT ALTERNATIVES FOR YOU

The feelings I have discussed are the most common ones that contribute to people staying emotionally attached to food during times of emotional upset. To make all of this even easier and clearer, I have included a feeling chart (see page 66). It is divided into the three sections covered in this chapter: feelings, needs, replacements. The suggested replacements are alternatives that many have found useful, but it is important that you feel free to come up with ideas and methods that work and fit your lifestyle. You can use this chart as a guide. Feel free to make up new replacements as you explore your particular emotional states. Also, maybe I left out some feelings. See if you can figure out what your needs might be and how you might fulfill them more directly without eating.

For every feeling you have used food to cope with, you can replace eating with a different, more positive behavior that will meet your emotional needs more closely and make you feel that much better about yourself. Meeting your emotional needs by arriving at your own inventive alternatives will feel wonderfully gratifying. It won't be long until, with continued practice, you will be your own bona fide feeling diagnostician and can come up with your own prescription for self-care. What-

ever new feelings surface, you will know how you need
to approach them and handle them.

## FEELING CHART

| Feeling | Need | Replacements |
| --- | --- | --- |
| Anger | Ventilation | Hit a pillow, scream and yell, write a letter |
| Hurt | Comfort | Hug a teddy bear, a pet, a friend |
| Boredom | Stimulation/ excitement | A trip into the city, a play, a class, boating; look into self |
| Guilt/remorse | Feeling unguilty/ off the hook | Look at act and find solution; avoid making a good/bad judgment |
| Tension | Relaxation | Bubble bath, massage, music, book, soap operas |
| Feeling trapped/ helpless | Feeling freer | Reinterpret situation, take a class, discuss feelings with a friend |
| Feeling inadequate | Feeling adequate | Get support from a friend, rational self-talk either silently or in a tape recorder |
| Feeling unattractive | Feeling attractive | Put on fresh makeup or shave, get a haircut or manicure, change clothes |

# 7
# Step 4:
# Making Sure Your
# Needs Get Met

By now you should be aware that activities that help satisfy your emotional needs are the best medicine to separate you from food's emotional ties. When you ignore these needs, cigarettes and, later, food beckon. You now know that healthier alternatives are available to fulfill these emotional needs.

But this awareness is only a part of the changing process. You must be willing to take action and implement some of the suggestions I have offered, as well as any of your own, into your daily life. For many, this "action" is the most difficult part of change.

For example, there was Anne, a thirty-year-old mother of a two-year-old. A school teacher, Anne had taken a leave of absence to be with her child. Anne really loved teaching and had not planned on quitting so soon. But when she became unexpectedly pregnant, she made the decision to stay home with her daughter. Her husband was doing well financially, so she didn't need to return to work for financial reasons. However, each afternoon as her daughter napped, she found herself in the kitchen, grazing from the pantry to the refrigerator. She knew she wasn't hungry, but she just kept eating.

As we began exploring her feelings, we discovered she was feeling unfulfilled and empty staying at home. She loved her child, but there was only so much baby talk she could talk. Yet, she felt guilty about her feelings. After all, she had a healthy child, and she "should" be content. Her guilt really blossomed when she considered her comfortable financial environment (though she did hate having to depend on her husband for her income) and her nice husband (though lately they never seemed to have any quality time together). Why, with everything she had, should she feel so empty?

Anne was another person with "rules" for how to be and feel. Anne's inner voice was screaming to her, "You need more!" Each time this voice shouted, Anne would turn a deaf ear. She was afraid that if she listened, she might abandon her child and go back to her other love, teaching. This wouldn't be a happy solution either.

To Anne, her choices were cut and dried, all or nothing. As we continued our sessions, we discussed what she could be doing to fulfill her needs, especially her need for more adult interaction. She and I began brainstorming. Anne wanted to go back to school for her master's degree. She decided to take one course a semester, and that would give her plenty of time to spend with her daughter. She also wanted some income of her own. She decided she would try to do some substitute teaching, so she began to search for a competent babysitter. She also knew she needed at least one afternoon or morning just for herself. So she contacted a neighbor and worked out a schedule to trade off their children every other day. As we probed and solved these issues, the grazing in the kitchen miraculously began to subside.

There was really no magic in what Anne and I did, but it did take some time and effort. You need to be willing to put in some work finding out what your emotional needs are, and then do whatever is necessary to ensure meeting those needs. A helpful technique is to list your top 10 needs. The list would look something like this:

I need more _____ in my life:

1.

2.

3.

4.

5.

6.

7.

8.

9.

10.

Then fill in the blanks. Sometimes this is easy. Perhaps you are already familiar with some of the things missing in your life. Good! At other times, you might need a bit more thought. That's OK; just sit down and do it. Write down whatever comes to your mind, anything that you feel is missing. Anne's list might have looked like this:

I need more _____ in my life:

1. *Intellectual stimulation*
2. *Fun*
3. *Relaxation*
4. *Alone time*
5. *Physical activity*
6. *Time with friends*
7. *Alone time with husband*
8. *My own income*
9. *Advanced education*
10. *Cultural stimulation*

After you make your list, draw a vertical line down the middle of the paper, and jot down how you might begin to meet your needs. Anne's might look like this:

**I need more _____ in my life:**

1. Intellectual stimulation
2. Fun
3. Relaxation
4. Alone time
5. Physical activity
6. Time with friends
7. Alone time with my husband
8. My own income
9. Advanced education
10. Cultural stimulation

**Here is how I am going to get more _____ in my life:**

1. Take a course
2. Tape soap operas
3. Take a bubble bath
4. Get sitter, go to library/mall
5. Walk or take exercise class
6. Start a children's play group
7. Get daughter to bed earlier; on Saturday night, get a sitter and go out to dinner
8. Substitute teach
9. Start master's program
10. Go to museum at least once a month

This exercise should help you become attuned to the needs in your life and how you can begin fulfilling them. But, because of our busy lives, we often wonder how we're going to find the time to take care of all our needs along with everyone else's. Sometimes it does seem hard to consider adding new dimensions to your life. But if you have time to eat and worry about your weight, you have time to address your self.

To make it easier to meet the needs you have listed, fill out a PUF (as in a magical "poof") chart. PUF stands for Putting You First. Many people are uncomfortable taking care of their emotional needs, as though they feel they don't deserve to be treated well. However, this rarely seems to be the case when it comes to taking care of everyone else's needs! Unfortunately, taking care of everyone else while ignoring oneself usually leads to anger, resentment, and self-pity. These feelings, in turn, lead many to food. Putting You First encourages you to take care of yourself *first*, so that you are more able to care for those around you. On an airplane, the flight attendant explaining the safety measures tells us to use the oxygen mask first (taking care of ourselves) and then to help our children. The more easily we breathe, the more capable we will be of assisting our children. So, strive for a balance between fulfilling your needs and responsibilities as well as caring for those around you. The goal here is not to exclude others but to *include* ourselves.

To use the PUF chart, start by making a list of your needs and how you might meet them. Feel free to use some of the ideas in the previous example, and add your own. Be creative! You know your lifestyle better than anyone else. After you have completed your list, on a separate sheet of paper make a list of your responsibilities. Remember that identifying your responsibilities is essential in formulating a positive self-image and a detachment from inappropriately using food, as well as fulfilling your emotional needs. This list might include work, grocery shopping, children, carpools, meetings, and errands. Upon completing both lists, you will be ready to fill in your self-care schedule.

The self-care schedule is a chart divided into squares, each representing a specific time of day. Fill in each square with either a responsibility or something that will help you meet one of your emotional needs. You can fill in a day's activities the evening before or a few days in advance. The purpose of the chart is to push you into being accountable to your entire being.

On pages 74–75, you will find an example of Anne's chart. Note that she has included plenty of time to be with her child, time to clean house, and time to do errands. But she has also included other things that she knows she needs for herself. She uses the chart as a tool to assist her in taking charge of herself.

A word of caution: try not to be too rigid with your time. For example, you know Sundays are always a particularly difficult day for you to avoid extra eating, so you plan a day of relaxing and watching television, and by some chance you receive a call from Robert Redford to meet for lunch. Go out with Bob! The chart is there as preventive medicine as well as a helper and guide. It ensures you will take care of your emotional self. If you know you tend to go for food every evening at 10:00 P.M., take a good look at what you really need at that hour. Is it comfort? If so, get out your teddy bear and hug away! Is it relaxation? Get the bubbles in the bath bubbling! Is it an outlet for anger or frustration? Get your Wiffle bat and start hitting! The thing you do not need is chocolate cake.

Anne's chart consists of three healthy meals a day, including a snack. Eating is an important part of everyone's day and a part of taking care of yourself. Now that you are emotionally detached from food, you will find it much easier to follow a reasonable eating plan such as the one offered in Chapter 9. It's OK to look forward to and enjoy your meals. Just remember, if food is on your mind constantly, it's a pretty good guess that you're neglecting something else.

One more comment about this PUF chart. Taking care of your needs on a daily basis can be scary. For example, if your inner voice has been telling you that you need more intimacy in your life and your spouse is unwilling or unable to meet those needs, other uncomfortable options are bound to pop into your head. Divorce, an affair, a fight, or marriage counseling are not alternatives most of us want to pursue. But whatever you discover about yourself and your needs has probably been plaguing you for a long time. Isn't it time to get everything out in the open and deal with it? Ignoring problems has been causing these unhealthy vices and your inability to effectively cope. The problems are still there, but on the periphery.

So do your chart. You're readying yourself to say your final good-bye to using food and smoking as a means of coping.

# ANNE'S SAMPLE PUF CHART

| | Monday | Tuesday | Wednesday | Thursday | Friday | Saturday | Sunday |
|---|---|---|---|---|---|---|---|
| **A.M.** | | | | | | | |
| 7:00–8:00 | Get up—dress Beth and me → | | | | | | |
| 8:00–9:00 | Have breakfast—read paper → | | | | | | |
| 9:00–10:00 | Exercise class | Grocery shopping | Exercise class | Play group | Exercise class | Family outing: park/zoo apple picking/movies → | Church → |
| 10:00–11:00 | Beth in nursery → | Bank and laundry → | Beth in nursery → | → | Beth in nursery → | | Visit parents → |
| 11:00–Noon | | | | | | Errands, laundry → | Leave Beth and |
| **P.M.** | | | | | | | |
| Noon–1:00 | Lunch → | | | | | | |
| 1:00–2:00 | Beth naps / Watch soaps | Clean | Afternoon out | Watch soaps | Clean → | → | |

| Time | | | | | | | |
|---|---|---|---|---|---|---|---|
| 2:00–3:00 | Read, sew | Study → | → | Read, knit | Study | Beth naps | go to Art Institute → |
| 3:00–4:00 | Beth up—take to park | | | Beth up—library | Beth up—mall | John and I alone | → |
| 4:00–5:00 | Rent tape | Study → | | Sesame Street | Sesame Street | John showers, Anne rests | |
| 5:00–6:00 | Make dinner / Beth play with plastic bowls ↑ | | | | | Anne showers, John rests | Pick up Beth |
| 6:00–7:00 | Eat dinner ↑ | | | | | Get sitter and go out → | Order in → |
| 7:00–8:00 | Clean up—John give Beth bath, read her story, put her to bed ↑ | | | | | | |
| 8:00–9:00 | Watch TV | Go to school → | Watch TV | Watch TV | Rent movie for us → | | Watch TV and relax → |
| 9:00–10:00 | Relax, phone calls | | Bubble bath | Read *People* magazine | | | |
| 10:00–11:00 | Be with John | | Be with John | Be with John | | | |
| 11:00 | Sleep | | | | | | |

# YOUR SAMPLE PUF CHART

|  | Monday | Tuesday | Wednesday | Thursday | Friday | Saturday | Sunday |
|---|---|---|---|---|---|---|---|
| **A.M.**<br>7:00–8:00 |  |  |  |  |  |  |  |
| 8:00–9:00 |  |  |  |  |  |  |  |
| 9:00–10:00 |  |  |  |  |  |  |  |
| 10:00–11:00 |  |  |  |  |  |  |  |
| 11:00–Noon |  |  |  |  |  |  |  |
| **P.M.**<br>Noon–1:00 |  |  |  |  |  |  |  |
| 1:00–2:00 |  |  |  |  |  |  |  |

| | | | | | |
|---|---|---|---|---|---|
| 2:00–3:00 | | | | | |
| 3:00–4:00 | | | | | |
| 4:00–5:00 | | | | | |
| 5:00–6:00 | | | | | |
| 6:00–7:00 | | | | | |
| 7:00–8:00 | | | | | |
| 8:00–9:00 | | | | | |
| 9:00–10:00 | | | | | |
| 10:00–11:00 | | | | | |
| 11:00 | | | | | |

# 8
# Step 5:
# The Mourning
# Process and the
# New You

By this time, it's probably very clear to you that your emotional attachment to food and cigarettes is due to unresolved problems and unmet needs. To break this vicious cycle, it's essential to address these feelings and needs directly, whether this be via hitting, hugging, taking a class, relabeling the situation, or whatever. Eating never resolves these issues.

But giving up something you have used as a source of comfort is very difficult. Many ex-smokers have described the process as like that of losing a good friend. One woman told me that even though she had quit smoking five years ago, she still had the habit of checking her purse to see if the cigarettes were there! Numerous people feel the same way about giving up unhampered eating. Therefore, it is important, as you ready yourself for the *I-Quit-Smoking Diet* eating plan, to go through a process of mourning the loss of both vices.

Here is one constructive way to mourn: get a large bag and call it your mourning bag. Fill it with the following items:

- *Anything in your closet that is too small or ugly that reminds you of your overeating or smoking self:* This means you need to go through your wardrobe and anything you feel fat in, anything that was a favorite "eating" outfit, goes in the bag. Throw away those loose sweat pants, old robe, or that favorite smoking jacket. Get rid of any reminders of the you that turned to unhealthy vices as a way to feel better.
- *All of your old "diet" books (except this one!):* You don't need detailed plans of what to eat, just the common-sense principles summarized in Chapter 8. Most diet books are filled with gimmicks and fads that are not only unhealthy, but encourage you to address only food as the answer to your "weight" problem, neglecting your emotional involvement. Seeking quick "remedies" to your problem is reminiscent of the old you.
- *A list of all your excuses and sayings:* Record your excuses such as, "I can't quit smoking because I'll gain so much weight," "I'll start my diet tomorrow," "I've already blown my diet, so I might as well eat everything in sight." All of these rationales apply to the symptoms but don't address the underlying issues. In the bag they go.
- *Old pictures:* Go through your old pictures and dig out any photos that show you smoking or eating. Throw out any photos of situations where you were eating too much—at a party, for example. Discard all the pictures that symbolize the "you" you want to change.
- *Old labels from food containers or cigarette packages:*

What are your favorite pigout foods? If when under emotional turmoil you grab for chocolate chip cookies, put the label from your favorite brand in the bag. Whatever type of cigarettes you smoked, put an old empty package in the bag. Gather as many as you can. Those labels will help you to see and feel your past behavior.

- *Other reminders:* If you can think of anything else that reminds you of the person who used smoking or food as a way of coping, put it in the bag. For example, a favorite lighter or an invitation to a party where you "pigged out" will do.

Putting this bag together should take only a bit of time, but be thorough. The contents should make an impact on you. After you have put most of it together, take some time to look through it. Examine what you have collected piece by piece. You should feel a certain amount of sadness as well as anger. If you don't feel anything, you have more work to do! As you inspect your gatherings, your feelings should be strong.

You are now ready to begin the mourning process. Each day, put aside five minutes to go through your bag. Put on soft music and really reflect. Saying good-bye to the part of your emotional self that abused food or cigarettes should bring on some sadness. While mourning, it is sometimes helpful to hold your teddy bear or any material object you find comfort in. As you go through each piece in your mourning bag, touch the article and remember how and when you inappropriately used it. Feel the time wasted as you ready yourself to say your final good-bye and start anew.

This mourning process is extremely helpful in pushing people to see how uncomfortable they were with their previous lifestyle. The more uncomfortable you are, the more apt you are to plunge into the deeper waters of change. Going through this bag should help you to feel a sense of sadness and emptiness, as well as anger for time lost. The stronger your feelings of loss, the more the odds are in your favor to avoid returning to unhealthy manners of coping.

Spend about a week going through this process. If you need more time, take it. Once you say good-bye to something dear to you, you can move on to forming new attachments. In this case, you will be readying yourself to formulate new ways to live your life. You will no longer use food to avoid confronting yourself and your problems. Feeling good about yourself means learning to handle these issues in new and healthier ways. To withdraw from yourself, your emotions, or your relationships means stagnation, lack of fulfillment, and the refrigerator.

Change can elicit feelings of discomfort. It's a part of growing up and maturing. Learning to tolerate ourselves and our imperfections allows us to live a more gratifying life. Taking a look at ourselves, our career, our relationships, our priorities, and choosing what our needs are contribute to a new sense of well-being. Anne's ideas of what "should" make her happy got her in trouble. This is a typical example of what happens to many of us. Realizing we have options, alternatives, and the ability to make up our own emotional "rules" keeps us from using unproductive coping strategies.

When you've completed the mourning process, go to the nearest garbage can and dump your bag. Make this action as symbolic as possible. Wear something new, and put on some new cologne. Remember, dumping the bag is not throwing away your entire persona, just the old parts of you that exercised unhealthy methods for coping with life. Dumping your bag is helping you redefine yourself and integrate new ideas and information into how you want to see yourself in the future.

When all of this is completed, it's time to put together a *New Me box*. It's often helpful and comforting, as you give up the old, to have something tangible to begin building the new. As the mourning bag represents old habits you want to discard, the New Me box will represent new ways you want to feel, look, and act. Put the following items in the New Me box:

- *A photograph:* This should be a picture (or pictures) that symbolizes how you would like to appear. It can be a magazine illustration or a picture of yourself at a particularly happy time in your life. Pick a photo based on more than appearance. It should be a photo of what the person embodies, an attitude that you admire and respect.
- *New sayings:* Write down inspirational thoughts on a scrap of paper, and pull it out when things get rough. The new you knows there will be various ups and downs and wants to be prepared. Reminders that are helpful might be: "When I feel anxious or uncomfortable, I will write down what happened and what I need," and, "I will always try to remember I have many options for dealing with every situation."
- *New goals:* Make a list of the kinds of things you would like to see yourself doing differently next year. Putting these thoughts in writing can increase the odds of you achieving what you want.
- *Reassess your values and priorities:* Many people are living by values they learned as children. Though some of these may be working quite well, some usually need some revamping. So take some time out to really think about what is important to you and in what order. If family is an important value but you

find yourself ignoring yours, explore what kind of changes might be needed. This exploration and reassessment is an important part of becoming the new you. List these priorities in order of importance, and put them in the box as well.

As with the mourning bag, take about five minutes a day to go through your New Me box. At this time, feel free to put on some lively music. As you go through each item in the box, see how you feel. Have you been doing things to take care of yourself as well as those around you? Does your appearance match how you want to feel? Have you been evaluating your values and priorities? Go through the box daily until you feel you've become the new you. At this point, it might be time to create another New Me box. Life is a series of changes, so feel free to retire this box and create a new one.

While you are mourning the old you and becoming the new you, you are bound to feel some hesitancy, even fear. It's kind of like learning to swim. Sometimes, you might feel you will never get the hang of it. But if you persist, you will and you'll soon love it. Likewise, if you stick with learning to change, the enjoyment will be worth the effort.

All in all, the new you will have three important principles to follow:

1. Be kind to yourself. Your needs are just as important as everyone else's. They're not necessarily *more* important, but *equally* important. Handling situations, thoughts, feelings, and needs with a commitment to self-nurturing is essential in formulating the new you.

2. If and when the desire to overeat occurs, stop, think,

and explore. Find new alternatives to ensure that the changing process will continue.

3. Set realistic goals. Success is the ability to make changes through action. Having a plan assists you in taking your mental awareness that extra mile. Set some goals and go for it!

As you put this three-part formula into action, you will quickly begin enjoying a new and more satisfying you. You will not only find greater enjoyment in being with others, but you will also find you love being with yourself. Knowing that you have imperfections but also great potential builds on the foundation of a strong self-image. A stronger foundation and less emotional attachment to food will make following the *I-Quit-Smoking Diet* eating plan comfortable and easy.

# 9
# Step 6:
# The *I-Quit-Smoking Diet* Eating Plan

Now that you are less emotionally attached to food, you're ready to learn what should be included in your eating plan to ensure weight stabilization and, if desired, weight loss. As mentioned in the first chapter, when smoking, your basic metabolic rate does increase. But the amount of increase—and, therefore, the decrease upon quitting—is not significant. If all other factors remain unchanged (if your eating habits and exercise levels do not fluctuate), any weight change will be very minor. People who gain weight upon quitting are usually substituting eating for smoking. They are looking for something to put in their mouth and ways to keep their hands busy. Combine this with a heightened sense of taste and smell, and food looks better and better to the ex-smoker! However, if you eat moderately, are aware of the emotional and psychological issues related to food, and do some form of moderate exercise (see Chapter 10), your weight should be fine.

This eating plan is based on the general principles of sound nutrition. According to the American Cancer Society, the following are all commonsense ways to approach food intake: eating less fat and more fruits, vegetables, and whole grains; avoiding foods with preservatives; and drinking very little alcohol. Also, carbohydrates, fats, vitamins, and minerals each have an important role in the diet. Once you understand these components of a healthy diet, you can make healthy choices a lifelong practice.

As an ex-smoker, you need to be more aware than ever of the impact good nutrition has on your life. Healthy eating will not only make your body run better, it will keep you from returning to unhealthy habits, like smoking. You'll be less likely to regress and inhale that first puff if you're feeling the best you've ever felt. By learning how to avoid fats and cholesterol in your diet, and acquainting yourself with which foods are high in vitamins, minerals, and fiber, I guarantee you'll be more careful about what you put in your body.

# CARBOHYDRATES

Until recently, carbohydrates have had a bad reputation. Associated with weight gain and tooth decay, carbohydrates were considered taboo to any serious dieter. In addition, historical factors aided the downfall of carbohydrates. During the Depression years, carbohydrates were the mainstay of the American diet, primarily because they were the cheapest source of food. However, as the economy improved, consumption of high-fat and high-protein foods became a sign of affluence, and the carbohydrate-based diet was abandoned by all but the lower classes. But in the past decade, the tables have turned, and the virtues of carbohydrates are being extolled from all sectors: nutritionists, doctors, athletes, and laypersons alike.

Just what are carbohydrates, and what is their role in human nutrition? Chemically, carbohydrates are composed of carbon, hydrogen, and oxygen combined to form a basic unit, or monosaccharide. These monosaccharides can exist singly, in pairs as disaccharides, or in long chains called polysaccharides. Generally the carbohydrates are divided into two classes: simple and complex. Simple carbohydrates are the mono- and disaccharides and include glucose and sucrose (common table sugar). Complex carbohydrates are the polysaccharides and include starches and fibers. However, once inside the body, almost all carbohydrates are converted to the monosaccharide glucose. Therefore, whether you eat an apple, some pasta, a piece of whole-wheat bread, or a candy bar, the carbohydrate in these foods will end up as the same product—glucose.

The principal role of carbohydrates in the body is to provide energy. In fact, carbohydrates are preferred over protein and fat as an energy source. If, however, the body is presented with both a protein and a carbohydrate for energy, it will use the carbohydrate for energy, allowing the protein to fulfill its intended function. Carbohydrates also function in "protein sparing." This means that when the diet lacks adequate carbohydrates, the body is forced to break down proteins to obtain energy. But this prevents proteins from fulfilling their intended functions, and deleterious consequences can result. You should therefore be wary of any diet that drastically reduces carbohydrate intake.

Almost all plant foods are good sources of carbohydrates. Animal foods are generally poor sources, with the exception of milk and milk products. Because plant foods (fruits, vegetables, grains) are so abundant, it is relatively easy to obtain adequate amounts of carbohydrates in your diet.

How should carbohydrate consumption be divided between simple and complex carbohydrates? Currently the typical American diet derives 25 percent of total calories from sugar and 25 percent from complex carbohydrates. However, according to Eleanor Noss Whitney and Eva May Hamilton in *Understanding Nutrition*, experts recommend that we instead consume only 10 percent of our daily calories in the form of sugar and close to 50 percent in the form of complex carbohydrates. Therefore, the emphasis in our diets should be on complex carbohydrates such as grains, potatoes, and legumes.

Emphasizing complex carbohydrates in your diet does not mean you should completely eliminate simple sugars. First of all, let's face it, they taste good. Trying to completely deprive yourself of sweets will probably only lead to a big binge later on. So keep some sugars in your diet; just reduce their frequency and serving size.

Because virtually all sugars are broken down or converted to glucose, whether you eat a candy bar, a dish of whole-grain cereal, or a vegetable, the carbohydrate it contains will end up as glucose. However, the simple sugars in the candy bar cause a rapid rise in blood glucose levels, causing you to feel a temporary "sugar high." But your insulin goes to work pulling glucose out of the blood, bringing glucose levels back to normal. Often, though, excess insulin is secreted, bringing blood glucose levels below normal and causing you to feel drained and sluggish. So although simple sugars can give you a quick burst of energy, over the long run they probably will make you feel more tired. In contrast, complex carbohydrates cause a slow, gradual rise in blood glucose levels, allowing you to avoid the extremes of the "sugar high" followed by the "sugar low."

Contrary to popular belief, sugar in and of itself is not unhealthy. Table sugar is composed of the two monosaccharides glucose and fructose, both of which provide energy for our bodies. However, the problem with sugar is that it is an "empty calorie food." This means that, while sugar provides calories, it supplies few essential nutrients such as protein, vitamins, and minerals. Complex carbohydrates, on the other hand, do provide needed nutrients along with their calories. Eating too much sugar can become a problem when it displaces foods with high nutrient values. If you eat a well-balanced diet containing the needed amounts of protein, vitamins, and minerals, you should have no problem with eating some sugary foods. But if your diet is not nutritionally sound, it could be because sugars are taking the place of the nutrient-rich foods your body needs.

Perhaps the biggest complaint voiced against sugar is that it is fattening. This simply is *not* true. All carbohydrates, simple and complex, contain only four calories per gram. Likewise, protein contains only four calories per gram. Fats are the food group that is fattening, providing nine calories per gram. Therefore, sugar alone doesn't make people fat, fat does. Unfortunately, many foods with high sugar content also contain a lot of fat—ice cream, candy, pie, cake, and cookies, to name a few. So when you choose to eat sweet-tasting, sugary foods you are also eating a good deal of fat. If you are watching your weight, remember that high-sugar, high-fat treats are also high in calories and should be eaten in moderation.

One component of carbohydrates that has received a great deal of favorable attention recently is fiber. Fiber is a substance found in plants that has a structure which prevents it from being digested by enzymes in the human body. Therefore, when eaten, fiber generally passes through the body unchanged and is virtually calorie-free.

Fiber has many health benefits that help to explain its recent popularity. First, fiber helps in weight control. Because it is indigestible, it is filling without adding many calories, causing the dieter to feel less hungry. Fiber also helps to prevent constipation by causing water to move into the digestive tract, softening the feces. More importantly, fiber helps to prevent some serious diseases. A diet high in fiber reduces a person's risk of diverticulosis, a weakening of the intestinal walls causing the formation of pouches that may become infected. Fiber reduces the risk of colon cancer by shortening the amount of time food remains in the digestive tract, therefore limiting the time that carcinogens in food come into contact with the body. Finally, fiber helps reduce the risk of cardiovascular disease, because it binds to cholesterol, causing the cholesterol to be excreted from the body. As you can see, fiber is important both in weight control and in disease prevention.

The best way to obtain adequate fiber is with a diet rich in plant foods. Good sources of fiber include legumes, whole grains and cereals, and fruits and vegetables. Unless advised by a doctor, avoid fiber supplements, because too much fiber is just as harmful as too little. Because fiber speeds up the transit time through the intestine, it allows less time for the proper absorption of essential nutrients, especially iron, calcium, potassium, and zinc. So obtain your fiber the natural way, through low-calorie, high-fiber foods, which offer many other nutritional benefits as well.

For smokers and ex-smokers, there are a few special concerns relating to carbohydrates. First, because smoking damages the body in a variety of ways, it is very important for the smoker to eat a well-balanced diet to keep the body functioning properly. This means consuming about 55 percent of your daily calories as carbohydrates, with the emphasis on the complex variety such as whole wheat breads, whole grain cereals, legumes, potatoes, and rice. In addition, because nicotine causes a smoker's blood glucose level to rise, quitting causes blood glucose levels to fall, so you may tend to prefer sweets and starches as your body attempts to elevate blood glucose to previous levels. Research by Neil Grunberg at the Uniformed Services University of the Health Sciences confirms this belief. In Grunberg's study, smokers, as well as rats injected with nicotine, chose a lower proportion of sweet foods than did nonsmokers, but they chose equal proportions of salty and bland foods. Moreover, after nicotine was withdrawn in the rats and humans, both groups tended to prefer sweet foods.

Fortunately, this natural craving for carbohydrates may actually aid you in your attempt to quit. A study by Deborah Bowen at the Fred Hutchinson Cancer Research Center found that ex-smokers fed a high-carbohydrate diet were less hostile and nervous and twice as successful in quitting as those fed a low-carbohydrate diet. As a result, it seems logical that you should follow your cravings for carbohydrates, since a high-carbohydrate diet will make quitting easier. Remember that as the body stabilizes, the cravings diminish.

# FATS

Like simple sugars, fats have a bad reputation. Besides contributing to obesity, high-fat diets are implicated in causing cancer and heart disease. But don't despair, fats do have some redeeming qualities and are an essential part of our diets. Some functions of dietary fat include providing energy to the body; carrying vitamins

A, D, E, and K; adding flavor and aroma to foods; and creating a feeling of fullness after eating. So fats aren't all bad, but unfortunately, most Americans consume fat in excess of need.

Most fat in our diets is in the form of triglycerides: a molecule of glycerol with three fatty acids attached to it. These fatty acids can be saturated or unsaturated. A saturated fatty acid is attached to as many hydrogen atoms as it can hold. A monounsaturated fatty acid is lacking two hydrogen atoms, while a polyunsaturated fatty acid lacks more than two hydrogen atoms. Thus, saturated fat is composed primarily of saturated fatty acids—a monounsaturated fat of monounsaturated fatty acids, and a polyunsaturated fat of polyunsaturated fatty acids. In foods, animal fats are usually saturated fats, olive and peanut oils are monounsaturated fats, while most other vegetable oils are polyunsaturated fats with the exception of palm oil and coconut oil. The American Heart Association recommends that fats constitute 30 percent of our daily calories, with about 10 percent coming from each type of fat. To reach this goal, most Americans would have to greatly reduce their intake of saturated fats while slightly increasing consumption of mono- and polyunsaturated fats.

The second type of fat prevalent in our diets is cholesterol. Cholesterol is essential to proper body functioning, but we don't require cholesterol in our diets because our bodies are able to manufacture all the cholesterol they need. Although cholesterol does serve some important functions, it becomes harmful to our bodies when it gets deposited on the walls of our arteries, often resulting in heart attacks or strokes. It is especially important for smokers and ex-smokers to maintain low blood cholesterol levels, because smoking and high blood cholesterol are two of the three major risk factors for heart disease.

Cholesterol is found *only* in animal foods; pure plant foods such as cereals, fruits, vegetables, breads made without animal fats, and even peanut butter are all cholesterol-free. In contrast, eggs, liver, and red meats are high in cholesterol. However, it is interesting to note that it is the saturated fat, not the cholesterol in foods, that has the greatest influence on blood cholesterol levels.

Besides saturated fats, another factor affecting cholesterol levels in the arteries is the type of lipoproteins present. Lipoproteins are the substances that transport fat throughout the body. Two of the four types of lipoproteins are low-density lipoproteins (LDLs) and high-density lipoproteins (HDLs). LDLs move throughout the body, depositing cholesterol in the body cells, including the cells of the heart. Therefore, high levels of LDLs are a major risk factor in heart disease. HDLs act in opposition to LDLs, removing cholesterol from the cells and returning it to the liver. So it follows that high levels of HDLs decrease the risk of heart disease.

Fortunately, there are ways to help increase your HDLs. The most effective method of raising HDL levels is to exercise regularly. The program outlined in the next chapter can help you start exercising in a way tailored to your needs and lifestyle. Quitting smoking also helps to raise HDL levels.

Other ways to reduce the cholesterol levels in your blood include consuming more fiber and fish. Increasing your fiber intake will reduce your blood cholesterol levels because fiber binds to cholesterol, causing it to be excreted from the body. You may have heard a lot of talk recently about certain fish oils that help prevent heart disease. These fish oils contain certain fatty acids that actually lower blood cholesterol levels. Because fish is a food source high in protein and low in fat, it makes sense to include more fish in your diet. The vari-

eties of fish most beneficial to reducing blood cholesterol levels are mackerel, herring, sardines, bluefish,
salmon, and tuna.

# VITAMINS AND MINERALS

Another important component of your diet is vitamins
and minerals. The table on this page summarizes the
functions and sources of the ones most important for
smokers and ex-smokers. Contrary to popular belief,
vitamins and minerals *do not* provide energy. I have
heard people say that they take a vitamin pill in order
to get more energy. Vitamins and minerals have no calories and therefore cannot provide energy. However,
vitamins and minerals are required for normal metabolism and in many energy-releasing reactions. Thus, a
vitamin deficiency may cause fatigue, but taking excess vitamins will not necessarily give you more
energy.

This brings up the issue of vitamin and mineral supplements. If you eat a well-balanced diet, you are probably getting the recommended daily allowance of vitamins and minerals. However, if you are trying to lose
weight, you may not be consuming enough food to provide the needed vitamins and minerals, so a daily multivitamin supplement may be advisable. But unless you
are under the direction of a physician, taking supplements of a single vitamin or mineral probably won't
help much and may be toxic if you consume megadoses.

The vitamins especially important for smokers and
ex-smokers are the B-complex vitamins and vitamins
C, E, and A. The B-complex vitamins have a multitude
of vital roles in body functioning, although unfortunately some of the vitamins are affected by smoking.
Studies reported on in *Science News* (December 1986)
show that the nitrous oxide in smoke breaks down vita-

## SUMMARY OF VITAMINS AND MINERALS

| Vitamin/Mineral | Function | Sources |
| --- | --- | --- |
| Folic acid/ Vitamin B$_{12}$ | Prevents lung cancer; calms nicotine deprived nerves | Meat, fish, eggs, milk, dark green leafy vegetables, wheat germ |
| Vitamin C | Antioxidant (combats cancer-causing oxidants in cigarette smoke) | Citrus fruits, cantaloupe, broccoli, strawberries, green pepper, brussels sprouts |
| Vitamin E | Antioxidant | Vegetable oils, margarine, whole grains, green leafy vegetables |
| Vitamin A | Maintains mucous membranes | Dark green, orange, and yellow fruits and vegetables (including broccoli, spinach, carrots, apricots, cantaloupe) |
| Selenium | Antioxidant, detoxifies heavy metals in smoke | Meat, fish, poultry, grains |
| Calcium | Prevents osteoporosis; reduces blood pressure | Dairy products (including milk, cheese, yogurt) |

min $B_{12}$ and that folic acid is also inactivated by smoking. Smoking reduces B-vitamin levels in the lungs, and these low levels are linked with lung cancer. B vitamins help calm nicotine-deprived nerves, making quitting less stressful. Thus, any diet for an ex-smoker should include many foods rich in B vitamins, such as lean meat, fish, eggs, low-fat milk, dark green leafy vegetables, and wheat germ.

According to information in Dr. Tom Ferguson's book *The Smoker's Book of Health*, vitamin C is another vitamin destroyed by smoking. In fact, vitamin C levels in the blood of smokers are 30 to 50 percent lower than in nonsmokers. This is unfortunate, because smokers have a greater need for vitamin C than nonsmokers. One of the functions of vitamin C is that it serves as an antioxidant, inhibiting the formation of cancer-causing nitrosamines. Because smokers are at an increased risk for lung cancer, it is especially important for them to get plenty of vitamin C. Good sources of vitamin C include citrus fruits, cantaloupe, strawberries, broccoli, green peppers, and brussels sprouts.

Another vitamin that serves as an antioxidant is vitamin E. Vitamin E helps protect both vitamin A from attack by oxygen, and the lung tissue from the harmful oxidants found in cigarette smoke. Research shows that smokers have less vitamin E in their lung fluid than nonsmokers, demonstrating that vitamin E is used up combating smoke oxidants. The good news for ex-smokers is that the combination of increasing vitamin E intake and decreasing oxidants inhaled will help bring the level of vitamin E in the lungs closer to normal. Good sources of vitamin E are vegetable oils, margarine, whole grains, and green leafy vegetables.

Vitamin A also has important implications for smokers. One of vitamin A's primary functions is to maintain the soundness of mucous membranes, including the lining of the lungs. Studies show that people with low amounts of vitamin A in their blood are more likely to develop cancer. Perhaps this is because the integrity of the mucous membranes lining the lungs has been compromised due to the lack of vitamin A, allowing carcinogens to more effectively invade the lung tissue. Currently the American Cancer Society suggests that a diet rich in vitamin A may help prevent cancer. Good food sources of vitamin A include dark green, orange, and yellow vegetables and fruits such as broccoli, spinach, carrots, apricots, and cantaloupe.

When considering the role of minerals in the diet, you should follow the same rule as for vitamins: more isn't necessarily better. Unless you are under the guidance of a physician, avoid taking supplements of a single mineral, because in excess, minerals too can be toxic. However, if you are on a calorie-restricted diet, taking a daily multivitamin and mineral supplement may be beneficial.

Although all the various minerals have important functions in the body, two have special implications for smokers: selenium and calcium. Selenium is a trace mineral, meaning it is required by the body in very, very small amounts. Selenium, like vitamins E and C, is an antioxidant that helps protect the cells of the respiratory tract from damage by the oxidants in cigarette smoke. In addition, selenium detoxifies heavy metals like mercury and cadmium, which are present in cigarette smoke. Because selenium is a trace mineral, you shouldn't need supplements. A well-balanced diet that includes adequate amounts of meat, fish, poultry, and grains should provide you with all the selenium your body requires.

Calcium, in contrast to selenium, is a major mineral, meaning the body requires it in greater amounts. The current recommended dietary allowance (RDA) of calcium for adults is 800 milligrams, whereas there is no RDA for selenium. Dairy products such as milk, cheese, and yogurt are all good sources of calcium. Lately calcium is being added to a wide variety of foods from cereal to orange juice to antacids because of its role in preventing the feared bone disease called osteoporosis.

Prevention of osteoporosis is one reason why smokers need to receive optimal amounts of calcium in their diets, for smoking has been found to increase the risk of osteoporosis. This does not mean that adequate amounts of dietary calcium will counteract the detrimental effects of smoking, but at least the calcium will help slow bone loss.

Another reason calcium is so important in a smoker's diet relates to blood pressure. Smoking has been found to increase a person's blood pressure by 10 to 15 percent. The carbon monoxide in smoke displaces some of the oxygen that the red blood cells normally transport throughout the body. Since there is less oxygen in the blood, the heart must beat harder and faster to deliver enough oxygen to the various organs, and this increases blood pressure. However, one of the functions of calcium is regulation of blood pressure. In fact, studies have found that the lower the levels of dietary calcium, the higher the blood pressure. So keeping blood pressure down is another reason why smokers should monitor their calcium intakes.

# PROTEIN

Many people think protein (and for many of us that means meat) is unhealthy. This is not altogether true. Protein is essential! The negative representation of protein and, more specifically, red meat is not about the protein that meat offers, but about the fat and cholesterol it also supplies. So as a protein source, meat is really quite good, but due to its high fat content and its unhealthy cholesterol levels, doctors wisely suggest we eat it in moderation.

Proteins as a class are diverse in terms of their structure and function. However, all proteins are similar in that they are composed of amino acids arranged into chains. There are 20 different amino acids, which are arranged into chains of varying sequences and lengths, yielding thousands of different proteins. These proteins have a wide variety of functions in the human body. They form enzymes, hormones, and antibodies, and they are an important structural component in tissues, especially muscles. (Please note that simply eating great quantities of protein will *not* make you more muscular. The only way to increase muscle size is through physical activity.) Proteins can also function as an energy source if sufficient carbohydrates and fats are unavailable. This explains why diets that severely restrict calories will cause the dieter to experience muscle loss. When the body cannot get enough energy from food, it is forced to break down lean muscle tissue to meet its energy needs. At the other extreme, any protein eaten in excess of need ultimately becomes body fat, so watch your portion sizes.

The United States RDA for protein is 0.8 grams per kilogram of body weight (1 kilogram equals 2.2 pounds). If you consume an appropriate diet, protein should constitute about 15 percent of your daily caloric intake. Good sources of protein include meats (beef, pork, lamb, chicken, and fish), eggs, and milk products (milk, cheese, and yogurt). In addition, some legumes, vegetables, nuts, and grains are also good protein sources when eaten in specific combinations. This system of combining nonmeat foods to obtain protein forms the basis of the vegetarian diet. But because this book provides only an overview of nutrition, it doesn't go into the details of vegetarianism. If you are currently a vegetarian or are contemplating becoming one, it is absolutely essential that you understand protein complementarity, and should therefore purchase some books on the subject or consult a Registered Dietitian.

## HOW THE EATING PLAN WORKS

A healthy balance of carbohydrates, fats, vitamins, and minerals provides the foundation for this eating plan. The plan has three basic components:

1. It includes foods to make the initial withdrawal from nicotine easier. As previously mentioned, nicotine leaves the body primarily via the kidneys, and if the urine is alkaline, the nicotine will leave in a more gradual manner. This results in a more constant level of nicotine in the blood. Without the sudden jolt of lack of nicotine, you will have fewer cravings for a cigarette. So the first week, if you really want to increase the odds of experiencing mild withdrawal, keep the urine as alkaline as possible.* Certain foods contribute to this alkaline process more than others. Foods that contain potassium, calcium, magnesium, and sodium are the best sources. These include all vegetables (except corn), all fruit juices (except cranberry, plum, and prune), and most milk products. Acid-forming foods to use moderately in the first week would include poultry, seafood (except shrimp), and eggs. Also, many smokers need more of vitamins C and B, so the diet plan includes foods rich in both these vitamins.

*One study suggests taking bicarbonate of soda to increase the alkaline state of the urine. This mixture is high in sodium, so anyone suffering high blood pressure, heart disease, or kidney problems *should not* drink this mixture. (Please check with your doctor.)

2. This program promotes a gradual weight loss of one to two pounds per week. If you do not want to lose weight but don't want to gain any, you may add larger portions. However, never decrease portions. Women of average height and weight should never consume under 800 calories, men, 1200.
3. This program provides an opportunity to create good lifetime eating habits. You can even have one ice-cream cone or two cookies a week, and your weight will not increase. The key word is *moderation*. If you eat reasonable portions, you can eat anything you want. There really are no taboo foods, only inappropriate amounts.

All in all, this eating plan is not radical. You shouldn't feel deprivation or denial. This is a well-balanced plan based on the four basic food groups (dairy products, grains, fruits and vegetables, and meat and legumes). By eating the recommended amounts of food from each of these groups, you can be sure that your diet won't be lacking in any essential vitamins and minerals.

The eating plan is presented as menus for three weeks' meals. Following the menus are two tables. One summarizes each of the four food groups, and the other is a list of exchanges. If you don't like a certain food on the menu or are unable to obtain it, simply make an appropriate substitution from the proper food group. Because your primary concern is to stay way from cigarettes while not overeating, your eating plan should be as enjoyable as possible. Therefore, don't hesitate to make changes in the menu. Just remember to keep your portions within the guidelines of the exchange list, and pay attention to your emotional state.

Each daily menu provides separate portions for men and women. In this diet, men are consuming a daily caloric intake of approximately 1,600 calories, whereas women are consuming 1,200 calories. These differences are attributed to the metabolism distinction between men and women.

One unique feature of this eating plan is that it includes a snack every day. These are foods that most other weight-loss diets forbid. But if we are honest with ourselves, these are the precise foods we crave when we want to cheat a little. Since I do not see food as the real issue, I have incorporated these ordinarily taboo foods daily. If you do not like the snack ideas offered, or if adding sugars or salts is difficult or a health problem, feel free to choose a more comfortable alternative. Try to keep your substitutions around 100–150 calories. You can eat these snacks once a day at any time.

On weekends, the snack listed is alcohol. One serving of alcohol means a light beer, a glass of wine, or one ounce of hard liquor. However, be aware that for many people, eating less or not smoking is difficult when drinking. Know thyself: if you feel you can have one drink without craving a cigarette or arousing your appetite, go ahead. If not, then substitute another snack on weekends and avoid alcohol altogether until you can handle it. (Caffeine also can lead you to backslide, so be cautious and use both sparingly. Your best bet is to drink lots of water, and avoid colas and other caffeinated products as much as possible.)

This eating plan includes a meal out. Obviously, you do not have to go out to dinner every weekend. If you would rather eat at home, fix a meal of your choice using the exchanges or borrowing a menu from one of the other days. Or if you would prefer to go out on a different night, just switch the meal plans. Eating out is fun and enjoyable. As always, you can eat what you want, just watch the portions.

Be careful to avoid playing some of the old mind games, like: "Well, eating out is so expensive, I'd better eat the whole thing. I would hate to waste my money, and besides, people are starving in Africa." To combat these old rationalizations that often accompany restaurant outings, think of your visit in this fashion: "Tonight I get to eat out. I don't have to cook or clean. So I am not just paying for the meal, I am paying for the service, too. I am also eating something I generally do not fix for myself. As far as finishing only half the food on my plate, that seems a better option than having it on my hips! After all, if we eat more than our bodies need, it becomes wasteful, unneeded fat. Better in the garbage!" Or, if throwing it away really goes against your grain, you can ask for a doggie bag and bring it home. But again, know thyself. If having it in the house is a threat to your staying on your eating plan, leave it at the restaurant. As for people starving in Africa, your steak really has no effect on them. If you feel horrible about their misfortune, feel free to send them a donation. So go out to dinner and enjoy the total experience!

Certain entries on the menus are marked with an asterisk. This means that a recipe has been included for that dish. The recipes follow the exchange table and are easy and delicious. Feel free to improvise and make up or add your own ideas. As long as you keep the exchange and calorie count balanced, you have a great deal of leeway.

After you finish the three-week plan, you can repeat the menus as long as you feel you need to use them. They offer enough variety so you shouldn't get bored. But if you do, substitute foods of your choice from the exchange table. And as with all new eating programs, check with your doctor before you begin.

# EATING PLAN MENUS

## Week 1 Day 1

**Breakfast**
2 pieces whole-wheat toast
1 cup skim milk
2 teaspoons margarine
Apple juice:
  —½ cup for women
  —1 cup for men
Coffee

**Lunch**
Chef's salad:
• Turkey:
  —1 ounce for women
  —2 ounces for men
• Carrots
• Green pepper
• Diet dressing:
  —2 tablespoons for
    women
  —3 tablespoons for men
Saltine crackers:
  —6 for women
  —9 for men
1 cup skim milk
Coffee, tea, diet soda, or
  water

**Snack**
10 potato chips

**Dinner**
Teriyaki Steak*:
  —3 ounces for women
  —4 ounces for men
3 ounces cooked spinach
Dinner roll:
  —1 for women
  —2 for men
Margarine:
  —1 teaspoon for women
  —2 teaspoons for men
¼ cantaloupe
Coffee, tea, diet soda, or
  water

**Diet Analysis**
Total calories:
  —Women 1,235
  —Men 1,603
46–52 percent carbohydrate
20–26 percent protein
28–34 percent fat

*Recipe on page 130

# Week 1 Day 2

**Breakfast**
¾ cup cold cereal
1 cup skim milk
Orange juice:
—½ cup for women
—1 cup for men
Coffee
*Men add:*
1 piece whole-wheat toast
1 teaspoon margarine

**Lunch**
Tuna salad sandwich:
• Tuna:
—2 ounces for women
—3 ounces for men
• Celery and onion
• Mayonnaise:
—2 teaspoons for women
—1 tablespoon for men
• 2 slices whole-wheat
bread
1 apple
1 cup skim milk
Coffee or diet soda

**Snack**
½ cup ice cream

**Dinner**
Baked or grilled Barbecue
Chicken*:
—3 ounces for women
—4 ounces for men
Cornbread:
—2-inch square piece for
women
—4-inch square piece for
men
½ cup asparagus
½ cup blueberries
Coffee, tea, diet soda, or
water

**Diet Analysis**
Total calories:
—Women 1,210
—Men 1,631
50–55 percent carbohydrate
21–26 percent protein
23–29 percent fat

*Recipe on page 130

# Week 1 Day 3

## Breakfast
¾ cup cold cereal
1 cup skim milk
½ grapefruit
Coffee
*Men add:*
   1 piece whole-wheat toast
   1 teaspoon margarine

## Lunch
Fruit salad plate:
- ½ cup cottage cheese
- 12 red grapes
- ¼ honeydew melon
- Peach

4 bread sticks
1 cup skim milk
Coffee, tea, diet soda, or
  water

## Snack
⅒ pound cake

## Dinner
Broccoli Quiche*:
  —⅛ for women
  —¼ for men
½ cup cooked cauliflower
1 hard roll
1 teaspoon margarine
Fruit cocktail:
  —½ cup for women
  —1 cup for men
Coffee, tea, diet soda, or
  water

## Diet Analysis
Total calories:
  —Women 1,238
  —Men 1,636
53–61 percent carbohydrate
16–21 percent protein
22–31 percent fat

*Recipe on page 131

# Week 1 Day 4

**Breakfast**
Scrambled eggs:
—1 for women
—2 for men
English muffin:
—½ for women
—1 for men
Margarine:
—1 teaspoon for women
—2 teaspoons for men
¾ cup strawberries
1 cup skim milk
Coffee

**Lunch**
5 ounces (condensed) New
England clam chowder
(add water)
24 oyster crackers
1 orange
Coffee, tea, diet soda, or
water
*Men add:*
1 blueberry muffin

**Snack**
2 chocolate chip cookies

**Dinner**
Chicken Parmesan*
½ cup noodles, cooked
1 teaspoon margarine
Salad:
• Lettuce
• Cucumber
• Tomato
• 1 tablespoon diet dressing
½ cup cranberry juice
Coffee, tea, diet soda, or
water
*Men add:*
¼ cup raisins

**Diet Analysis**
Total calories:
—Women 1,171
—Men 1,591
51–55 percent carbohydrate
14–17 percent protein
31–34 percent fat

*Recipe on page 132

# Week 1 Day 5

**Breakfast**
¾ cup cold cereal
1 cup skim milk
1 banana
Coffee
*Men add:*
　½ cup orange juice

**Lunch**
Roast beef sandwich:
- Roast beef:
　—1 ounce for women
　—2 ounces for men
- Mayonnaise:
　—1 teaspoon for women
　—2 teaspoons for men
- Lettuce
- Whole-wheat bread:
　—1 slice for women
　—2 slices for men
Bran muffin:
　—½ for women
　—1 for men
1 cup skim milk
1 plum
Coffee, tea, diet soda, or
　water

**Snack**
12 ounces light beer, 5
　ounces wine, or 1 ounce
　hard liquor

**Dinner**
Sole with Dill Sauce*
Baked potato
2 teaspoons margarine
½ cup broccoli
Coffee, tea, diet soda, or
　water
*Men add:*
　1 apple

**Diet Analysis**
Total calories:
　—Women 1,197
　—Men 1,610
50–57 percent carbohydrate
19–26 percent protein
24–29 percent fat

*Recipe on page 133

# Week 1 Day 6

**Breakfast**
1 bagel
1 ounce cream cheese
1 cup skim milk
Grapefruit juice:
—½ cup for women
—1 cup for men
Coffee
*Men add:*
10 cherries

**Lunch**
1 8-ounce container yogurt
4 Triscuit crackers
12 grapes
1 cup watermelon
Coffee, tea, diet soda, or
water
*Men add:*
1 slice whole-wheat bread
1 tablespoon peanut
butter

**Snack**
12 ounces light beer, 5
ounces wine, or 1 ounce
hard liquor

**Dinner**
Dinner out, include:
• 3 ounces lean meat, fish,
or poultry
• 1 bread
• 2 teaspoons fat (sour
cream, margarine,
mayonnaise, or salad
dressing)
• 1 vegetable
Coffee, tea, diet soda, or
water

**Diet Analysis**
Total calories:
—Women 1,187
—Men 1,582
52–58 percent carbohydrate
16–22 percent protein
26–30 percent fat

# Week 1 Day 7

**Breakfast**
Fruit salad:
- Banana:
  —½ for women
  —1 for men
- ¾ cup strawberries
1 cup skim milk
Coffee
*Men add:*
  2 pieces whole-wheat toast
  2 teaspoons margarine

**Lunch**
PBJ:
- 1 tablespoon peanut butter
- 1 tablespoon jelly
- 2 slices bread
5 ounces (condensed) tomato soup (add water)
6 saltines
Coffee, tea, diet soda, or water
*Men add:*
  1 cup skim milk

**Snack**
1 ounce pretzels

**Dinner**
Shrimp with Mandarin Oranges*
Rice:
  —½ cup for women
  —¾ cup for men
½ cup broccoli
½ cup pineapple
Coffee, tea, diet soda, or water

**Diet Analysis**
Total calories:
  —Women 1,205
  —Men 1,622
66–71 percent carbohydrate
19–24 percent protein
9–15 percent fat

*Recipe on page 133

# Week 2 Day 1

## Breakfast
¾ cup cold cereal
1 cup skim milk
½ cup blueberries
Apple juice:
   —½ cup for women
   —1 cup for men
Coffee
*Men add:*
   1 piece whole-wheat toast
   1 teaspoon margarine

## Lunch
Turkey sandwich:
- Turkey:
   —2 ounces for women
   —4 ounces for men
- Mayonnaise:
   —1 teaspoon for women
   —2 teaspoons for men
- Lettuce and tomato
- 2 slices whole-wheat bread
1 orange
1 cup skim milk
Coffee, tea, diet soda, or
   water

## Snack
5 vanilla wafers

## Dinner
¼ cheese pizza
Salad:
- Lettuce
- Carrots
- Celery
- Tomato
- 1 tablespoon diet dressing
Coffee, tea, diet soda, or
   water
*Men add:*
   1 peach

## Diet Analysis
Total calories:
   —Women 1,217
   —Men 1,593
57–62 percent carbohydrate
19–23 percent protein
18–24 percent fat

# Week 2 Day 2

**Breakfast**
2 pieces whole-wheat toast
2 teaspoons margarine
1 cup skim milk
Orange juice:
　—½ cup for women
　—1 cup for men
Coffee

**Lunch**
1 8-ounce container yogurt
1 pear
Coffee, tea, diet soda, or
　water
*Men add:*
　1 corn muffin

**Snack**
1 1¾-inch square brownie

**Dinner**
Hamburger:
　—3 ounces for women
　—4 ounces for men
• Condiments
• Lettuce and tomato
• 1 hamburger bun
½ cup cabbage (raw)
1 tablespoon dressing*
Coffee, tea, diet soda, or
　water
*Men add:*
　1 apple

**Diet Analysis**
Total calories:
　—Women 1,268
　—Men 1,648
48–55 percent carbohydrate
15–19 percent protein
30–36 percent fat

*Recipe on page 139

# Week 2 Day 3

**Breakfast**
Scrambled eggs:
   —1 for women
   —2 for men
Whole-wheat toast:
   —1 piece for women
   —2 pieces for men
Margarine:
   —1 teaspoon for women
   —2 teaspoons for men
1 cup skim milk
Apple juice:
   —½ cup for women
   —1 cup for men
Coffee

**Lunch**
Pasta salad:
• Pasta:
   —1 cup for women
   —1½ cups for men
• Broccoli
• Carrots
• Diet dressing:
   —2 tablespoons for
    women
   —3 tablespoons for men
1 cup skim milk
¾ cup strawberries
Coffee, tea, diet soda, or
   water

**Snack**
1/12 angel food cake

**Dinner**
Scrod with Italian
   Dressing*
Baked potato
2 teaspoons margarine
½ cup brussels sprouts
Coffee, tea, diet soda, or
   water
*Men add:*
   ½ banana

**Diet Analysis**
Total calories:
   —Women 1,225
   —Men 1,638
55–61 percent carbohydrate
19–25 percent protein
20–24 percent fat

*Recipe on page 134

# Week 2 Day 4

## Breakfast
¾ cup cold cereal
1 cup skim milk
1 banana
Coffee
*Men add:*
    1 piece whole-wheat toast
    1 teaspoon margarine

## Lunch
Fruit salad plate:
• ½ cup cottage cheese
• 12 red grapes
• ¼ honeydew melon
• ¼ cantaloupe
4 bread sticks
Coffee, tea, diet soda, or
    water
*Men add:*
    1 plum
    1 cup skim milk

## Snack
1 1-ounce chocolate bar

## Dinner
Fettuccine and Vegetables*
Carrot and celery sticks
Coffee, tea, diet soda, or
    water
*Men add:*
1 piece garlic bread (1 slice
    of Italian bread with 1
    teaspoon margarine and
    garlic powder to taste)

## Diet Analysis
Total calories:
    —Women 1,240
    —Men 1,616
55–60 percent carbohydrate
18–20 percent protein
22–27 percent fat

*Recipe on page 135

# Week 2 Day 5

**Breakfast**
1 English muffin
2 teaspoons margarine
1 cup skim milk
Grapefruit:
—½ for women
—1 for men
Coffee

**Lunch**
Chef's salad:
• 1 hard-boiled egg
• Green pepper
• Lettuce
• Celery
• Cucumber
• Tomato
• Diet dressing:
—2 tablespoons for
women
—3 tablespoons for men
Wheat crackers:
—5 for women
—10 for men
1 cup skim milk
Coffee, tea, diet soda, or
water
*Men add:*
1 ounce cheese

**Snack**
12 ounces light beer, 5
ounces wine, or 1 ounce
hard liquor

**Dinner**
Bisquick Oven-Fried
Chicken*
1 biscuit
2 teaspoons margarine
3 ounces peas
Coffee, tea, diet soda, or
water

**Diet Analysis**
Total calories:
—Women 1,239
—Men 1,604
47–53 percent carbohydrate
21–27 percent protein
26–31 percent fat

*Recipe on page 135

# Week 2 Day 6

**Breakfast**
¾ cup cold cereal
1 cup skim milk
Orange juice:
—½ cup for women
—1 cup for men
1 peach
Coffee

**Lunch**
BLT:
• Bacon:
  —3 slices for women
  —4 slices for men
• Lettuce
• Tomato slices
• Mayonnaise:
  —1 teaspoon for women
  —2 teaspoons for men
• 2 pieces white toast
1 apple
1 cup skim milk
Coffee, tea, diet soda, or
  water
*Men add:*
  1 blueberry muffin

**Snack**
12 ounces light beer, 5
  ounces wine, or 1 ounce
  hard liquor

**Dinner**
Dinner out, include:
• 3 ounces lean meat, fish,
  or poultry
• 1 bread
• 2 teaspoons fat (sour
  cream, margarine, salad
  dressing, or mayonnaise)
• 1 vegetable
Coffee, tea, diet soda, or
  water

**Diet Analysis**
Total calories:
—Women 1,175
—Men 1,563
50–57 percent carbohydrate
19–25 percent protein
24–29 percent fat

# Week 2 Day 7

**Breakfast**
Poached eggs:
  —1 for women
  —2 for men
Whole-wheat toast:
  —1 piece for women
  —2 pieces for men
1 cup skim milk
Orange juice:
  —½ cup for women
  —1 cup for men
Coffee

**Lunch**
1½ cup spaghetti
Tomato sauce:
  —4 ounces for women
  —6 ounces for men
½ cup applesauce,
  unsweetened
1 cup skim milk
Coffee or diet soda

**Snack**
1 ounce pretzels

**Dinner**
Quick Chicken and
  Vegetable Stir-Fry*
Rice:
  —½ cup for women
  —¾ cup for men
Unsweetened pineapple:
  —½ cup for women
  —1 cup for men
Coffee, tea, diet soda, or
  water

**Diet Analysis**
Total calories:
  —Women 1,253
  —Men 1,608
58-64 percent carbohydrate
22-29 percent protein
13-29 percent fat

*Recipe on page 136

# Week 3 Day 1

## Breakfast
¾ cup cold cereal
1 cup skim milk
Grapefruit juice:
   —½ cup for women
   —1 cup for men
Coffee

## Lunch
Chicken salad sandwich:
- 2 ounces chicken
- 2 teaspoons mayonnaise
- Celery and onion
- 2 slices whole-wheat bread
1 cup skim milk
10 cherries
Coffee, tea, diet soda, or water

## Snack
2 cups unbuttered popcorn

## Dinner
Tacos:
- Ground beef prepared with taco mix:
   —2 ounces for women
   —4 ounces for men
- Cheese:
   —1 ounce for women
   —2 ounces for men
- Tomato, lettuce, and onion
- Taco shells:
   —1 for women
   —2 for men
3 ounces corn
1 pear
Coffee, tea, diet soda, or water

## Diet Analysis
Total calories:
   —Women 1,227
   —Men 1,617
46–55 percent carbohydrate
21–26 percent protein
24–32 percent fat

# Week 3 Day 2

**Breakfast**
Scrambled eggs:
—1 for women
—2 for men
Whole-wheat toast:
—1 piece for women
—2 pieces for men
Margarine:
—1 teaspoon for women
—2 teaspoons for men
1 cup skim milk
Cranberry juice:
—½ cup for women
—1 cup for men
Coffee

**Lunch**
Tossed salad:
• Lettuce
• Tomato
• Green pepper
• Cucumber
• 2 tablespoons diet
dressing
1 bran muffin
1 orange
Coffee, tea, diet soda, or
water
*Men add:*
1 ounce cheese

**Snack**
½ cup ice cream

**Dinner**
Chicken in Wine*
1 hard roll
1 teaspoon margarine
½ cup cooked carrots
Coffee, tea, diet soda, or
water
*Men add:*
½ cup unsweetened fruit
cocktail

**Diet Analysis**
Total calories:
—Women 1,234
—Men 1,642
47–50 percent carbohydrate
20–23 percent protein
29–33 percent fat

*Recipe on pages 136–37

# Week 3 Day 3

**Breakfast**
¾ cup cold cereal
1 cup skim milk
Orange juice:
—½ cup for women
—1 cup for men
Coffee

**Lunch**
1 8-ounce container yogurt
5 graham crackers
Raisins:
—2 tablespoons for
women
—¼ cup for men
Coffee, tea, diet soda, or
water
*Men add:*
1 corn muffin
2 teaspoons margarine

**Snack**
2 Oreo cookies

**Dinner**
1 3-ounce lean pork chop,
baked
Fresh Green Beans
Parmesan*
Baked potato
2 teaspoons margarine
½ cup unsweetened
applesauce
Coffee, tea, diet soda, or
water

**Diet Analysis**
Total calories:
—Women 1,259
—Men 1,626
53–60 percent carbohydrate
13–17 percent protein
27–32 percent fat

*Recipe on page 139

# Week 3 Day 4

**Breakfast**
Poached eggs:
—1 for women
—2 for men
Whole-wheat toast:
—1 piece for women
—2 pieces for men
1 cup skim milk
¼ cantaloupe
Coffee

**Lunch**
Pasta salad:
• Pasta:
—1 cup for women
—1½ cups for men
• Broccoli
• Carrots
• Diet dressing:
—2 tablespoons for
women
—3 tablespoons for men
1 cup skim milk
1 cup watermelon
Coffee, tea, diet soda, or
water

**Snack**
10 potato chips

**Dinner**
Salmon with Dijon
Mustard*
1 dinner roll
2 teaspoons margarine
½ cup mixed vegetables
1 cup apple juice
Coffee, tea, diet soda, or
water
*Men add:*
½ banana

**Diet Analysis**
Total calories:
—Women 1,214
—Men 1,607
52–57 percent carbohydrate
20–25 percent protein
23–28 percent fat

*Recipe on page 134

# Week 3 Day 5

**Breakfast**
Bagel:
—½ for women
—1 for men
Cream cheese:
—½ ounce for women
—1 ounce for men
1 cup skim milk
Orange juice:
—½ cup for women
—1 cup for men
Coffee

**Lunch**
Corned beef sandwich:
• Corned beef (lean):
—2 ounces for women
—3 ounces for men
• Mustard
• 2 slices rye bread
½ grapefruit
1 cup skim milk
Coffee, tea, diet soda, or
water

**Snack**
12 ounces light beer, 5
ounces wine, or 1 ounce
hard liquor

**Dinner**
Special Chicken
Drumsticks*
1 2-inch square piece
cornbread
2 teaspoons margarine
Tomato and cucumber slices
Coffee, tea, diet soda, or
water

**Diet Analysis**
Total calories:
—Women 1,257
—Men 1,647
42–46 percent carbohydrate
22–27 percent protein
31–36 percent fat

*Recipe on page 137

# Week 3 Day 6

**Breakfast**
¾ cup cold cereal
1 cup skim milk
1 banana
Coffee
*Men add:*
   1 piece whole-wheat toast
   1 teaspoon margarine
   ½ cup grapefruit juice

**Lunch**
Stir-Fried Broccoli*
Rice:
   —½ cup for women
   —¾ cup for men
5 wheat crackers
Cheese:
   —1 ounce for women
   —2 ounces for men
12 grapes
1 cup skim milk
Coffee, tea, diet soda, or
   water

**Snack**
12 ounces light beer, 5
   ounces wine, or 1 ounce
   hard liquor

**Dinner**
Dinner out, include:
• 3 ounces lean meat, fish,
   or poultry
• 1 bread
• 2 teaspoons fat (sour
   cream, margarine, salad
   dressing, or mayonnaise)
• 1 vegetable
   Coffee, tea, diet soda, or
   water

**Diet Analysis**
Total calories:
   —Women 1,218
   —Men 1,631
52–57 percent carbohydrate
21–27 percent protein
20–27 percent fat

*Recipe on page 140

# Week 3 Day 7

**Breakfast**
Whole-wheat toast:
—1 piece for women
—2 pieces for men
Margarine:
—1 teaspoon for women
—2 teaspoons for men
1 cup skim milk
½ cup orange juice
Coffee

**Lunch**
Grilled cheese sandwich:
• 2 slices bread
• 2 ounces cheese
• 1 teaspoon margarine
Small can V-8 juice
Coffee, tea, diet soda, or
water
*Men add:*
1 apple
5 ounces (condensed) cream
of chicken soup (add
water)

**Snack**
1 ounce jelly beans

**Dinner**
Lasagna with Spinach*
Fruit salad:
• 1 peach
• 1 plum
Coffee, tea, diet soda, or
water

**Diet Analysis**
Total calories:
—Women 1,253
—Men 1,656
52–58 percent carbohydrate
16–23 percent protein
25–31 percent fat

*Recipe on page 138

## BASIC FOOD GROUPS

| | Milk Group | Meat Group | Fruit and Vegetable Group | Grain Group |
|---|---|---|---|---|
| Number of servings daily | 2 | 2 | 4 | 4 |
| Major nutrients provided | Calcium, riboflavin, protein | Protein, niacin, iron, thiamin | Vitamin A, Vitamin C | Carbohydrates, thiamin, iron, niacin |
| Examples | Milk, yogurt, cheeses | Meat, fish, poultry, eggs, cheeses, peanut butter, legumes | Raw or cooked fruits and vegetables, juices | Bread, cereal, pasta |

# EXCHANGE LIST

## 1 Fruit Serving
½ cup juice:
- apple
- orange
- grapefruit
- cranberry

¼ cantaloupe
1 apple
½ cup blueberries
½ grapefruit
½ banana
12 grapes
¼ honeydew
1 peach
¾ cup strawberries
1 orange
2 tablespoons raisins
1 plum
1 cup watermelon
½ cup unsweetened applesauce
½ cup pineapple
1 pear
10 cherries
½ cup unsweetened fruit
   cocktail

## 1 Vegetable Serving
½ cup spinach
½ cup asparagus
½ cup cauliflower
½ cup broccoli
½ cup tomato
½ cup cabbage
½ cup brussels sprouts
½ cup carrots
½ cup green beans

## Vegetables *(cont'd)*
½ cup mixed vegetables
Free vegetable snacks:
- Lettuce
- Celery
- Cucumber
- Carrot sticks
- Radishes

## 1 Bread Serving
1 slice whole-wheat bread
1 slice white bread
1 slice rye bread
6 saltines
1 dinner roll
1 hard roll
¾ cup cold cereal
1 2-inch square piece
   cornbread
4 breadsticks
½ English muffin
24 oyster crackers
½ small muffin (bran, corn, or
   blueberry)
1 baked potato
½ bagel
½ cup cooked pasta
½ cup cooked rice
½ hamburger roll
½ hot dog bun
5 wheat crackers
1 biscuit
1 tortilla shell
5 graham crackers

## 1 Meat Serving

Lean:
- 1 ounce lean beef, lamb, or pork
- 1 ounce poultry
- 1 ounce fish or seafood
- ⅓ cup lowfat cottage cheese

Medium fat:
- 1 ounce 15 percent fat beef, lamb, or pork
- 1 egg
- 1 tablespoon peanut butter

High fat:
- 1 ounce 20 percent (or more) fat beef, lamb, or pork
- 1 ounce hard cheddar-type cheese
- 1 ounce cold cuts
- 1 hot dog

## 1 Fat Serving

1 teaspoon:
- cream cheese
- peanut butter
- butter
- margarine
- vegetable oil
- salad dressing (non-dietetic)

## 1 Milk Serving

1 cup skim milk**

## 1 Snack

10 potato chips
½ cup ice cream
⅒ pound cake
2 cookies
- Chocolate chip
- Oatmeal
- Peanut butter
- Shortbread
- Sugar

5 butter cookies
2 cups unbuttered popcorn
5 vanilla wafers
1¾-inch square brownie
1/12 angel food cake
1 1-ounce candy bar
1 ounce pretzels
1 ounce jelly beans
1 ounce hard candy
1 ounce nuts (any kind)
1 ounce corn chips
1 ounce tortilla chips
1 cupcake
1 granola bar
2 ounces cheesecake

For cereal breakfasts, try the following low-sugar cereals:
All Bran*
Cheerios
Cornflakes
Grape Nuts*
Nutri Grain*
Product 19
Raisin Bran*
Special K

---

*Highest in fiber.
**If you absolutely cannot tolerate skim milk, then drink 2 percent, which has only 30 calories more per serving, or eat 1 ounce of hard cheese or 4 ounces of low-fat yogurt.

# RECIPES

## TERIYAKI STEAK

3 tablespoons teriyaki sauce
3 tablespoons cooking wine
  Salt and pepper to taste
1 teaspoon garlic powder
2 tablespoons water
6 ounces filet or sirloin, raw

Combine all ingredients but meat. Pour sauce over steak and marinate for 2 hours. Grill or broil to taste.

*Serves 2.*

## BARBEQUE CHICKEN

2 tablespoons Open Pit barbeque sauce
  Freshly ground pepper or garlic
    powder
1-1½-pound broiler-fryer, cut into serving
    size pieces

Combine barbeque sauce and seasoning to taste. Brush chicken pieces with sauce. Grill or bake at 350°F until done, approximately 40 minutes.

*Serves 2-3.*

## BROCCOLI QUICHE

1 frozen 8-inch pie crust
4 ounces fresh broccoli, cut small
3 eggs
1 cup half and half
¾ cup skim milk
¾ teaspoon salt
Pinch pepper
3½ ounces Lorraine Swiss cheese
¾ ounce Parmesan cheese, grated

Bake pie crust as directed on package. Preheat oven to 375°F.

Cook broccoli until barely tender. Drain and squeeze out as much water as possible with paper towels.

Beat eggs. Add half and half, milk, seasonings, cheeses, and broccoli. Pour this mixture into baked pie crust. Bake at 375°F for 40 minutes.

*Serves 8.*

## CHICKEN PARMESAN

**Pepper**
¼ **teaspoon garlic powder**
¼ **teaspoon paprika**
1 **tablespoon parsley flakes**
¼ **cup grated Parmesan cheese**
⅓ **cup fine bread crumbs**
4 **4-ounce boneless chicken breasts**
⅓ **cup water**
1 **tablespoon vegetable oil**
¼ **cup melted margarine**
⅓ **cup marsala wine**

Preheat oven to 350°F. Combine seasonings, cheese, and bread crumbs in a plastic bag. Coat the chicken with this mixture by placing the chicken in the bag and shaking.

Put the water in a roasting pan, then arrange the chicken in the pan. Pour the oil and margarine over the chicken. Bake uncovered at 350°F for 30 minutes.

Pour wine over the chicken. Cover the pan with foil. Bake for 15 more minutes at 325°F.

Remove foil and bake for 10 more minutes at 350°F.

*Serves 4.*

## SOLE WITH DILL SAUCE

3 ounces fillet of sole
2 tablespoons plain yogurt
1 chopped scallion
⅛ teaspoon dried dill
   Salt and pepper to taste
1 teaspoon grated parmesan cheese

Place sole in a foil-lined 8″ × 8″ baking dish. Mix yogurt, scallion, dill, salt, and pepper in a small bowl. Spread over fish and sprinkle with cheese. Cover fish with aluminum foil and bake at 350°F for 15–20 minutes or until fish flakes.

*Serves 1.*

## SHRIMP WITH MANDARIN ORANGES

¼ cup beef broth
4 ounces cooked shrimp
½ cup low-calorie mandarin orange
   slices
¼ teaspoon salt
1 packet Sweet'n Low
½ green pepper, sliced
1 teaspoon cornstarch
2 teaspoons dry sherry

Heat broth in a 7-inch skillet. Add shrimp, oranges, salt, Sweet'n Low, and green papper. Heat through, stirring quickly, 1–2 minutes. Dissolve cornstarch in sherry. Add sherry mixture to other ingredients and heat through.

*Serves 1.*

## SALMON WITH DIJON MUSTARD

*Women:*
    3 ounces skinned and boned salmon
       steaks
    2 teaspoons Dijon mustard
*Men:*
    4 ounces skinned and boned salmon
       steaks
    1 tablespoon Dijon mustard

Barely cover the bottom of a baking pan with water.
Place salmon in pan. Broil a few minutes, until top of
salmon turns pink to brown. Turn salmon over and
spread mustard on top. Broil 3–5 minutes or until fish
flakes.

*Serves 1.*


## SCROD WITH ITALIAN DRESSING

    1 3-ounce scrod fillet
    1 tablespoon low-calorie Italian dressing
      Salt and pepper to taste
    ⅛ teaspoon garlic powder

Lay fish in an 8″ × 8″ baking dish. Top with dressing
and seasonings. Cover with aluminum foil and bake at
350°F for 20 minutes or until fish flakes.

*Serves 1.*

## FETTUCCINE AND VEGETABLES

**½ cup fettuccine noodles, cooked**
**½ cup cooked baby carrots**
**½ cup cooked snow peas**
**½ cup cooked mushrooms**
**2 ounces grated Parmesan cheese**
**2 tablespoons instant nonfat dry milk**
**Dash imitation butter flavor**
**Salt and pepper to taste**

Combine noodles and vegetables in the top of a double boiler. Add half of the cheese, and the dry milk and butter flavor. Stir, then add the rest of the cheese. Cook until cheese is melted. Season with salt and pepper.

*Serves 1.*

## BISQUICK OVEN-FRIED CHICKEN

**1 teaspoon margarine**
**2 tablespoons Bisquick baking mix**
**Paprika to taste**
**Salt and pepper to taste**
**3 ounces chicken**

Preheat oven to 425°F. Melt margarine in a small saucepan. In a separate bowl, mix baking mix, paprika, salt, and pepper; coat chicken. Place chicken in an 8″ × 8″ baking dish. Bake uncovered at 425°F for approximately 30 minutes, turning chicken every 15 minutes.

*Serves 1.*

## QUICK CHICKEN AND VEGETABLE STIR-FRY

¼ cup chicken broth
3 ounces chicken, thinly sliced
1 small green pepper, sliced
¼ cup fresh mushrooms, sliced
¼ cup onion, sliced
2 tablespoons soy sauce (light or dark)
2 teaspoons Sweet'n Low
¼ teaspoon ginger
1 teaspoon cornstarch
2 tablespoons beef broth

Heat chicken broth in nonstick skillet and add chicken; stir-fry quickly for 5–8 minutes, or until chicken turns white. Add vegetables and heat through 1–2 minutes. Combine soy sauce, Sweet'n Low, and ginger; pour over chicken mixture and heat through. Dissolve cornstarch in beef broth, and add to chicken mixture, stirring until sauce becomes thickened.

*Serves 1.*

## CHICKEN IN WINE

1 pound skinless breast of chicken
   (4 half-breasts)
2 tablespoons flour
2 tablespoons margarine
½ teaspoon salt
¼ teaspoon pepper
½ teaspoon garlic powder
¼ cup dry sherry

Wash chicken and pat dry. Pound chicken with mallet or rolling pin until thin. Sprinkle both sides of chicken with flour. In large skillet, melt margarine over medium heat; add chicken breasts and brown 2–3 minutes on each side. Lower heat, and add seasonings and sherry. Cover and simmer 5 minutes.

*Serves 4.*

## SPECIAL CHICKEN DRUMSTICKS

8 **chicken drumsticks**
2 **tablespoons orange juice**
¼ **cup herb stuffing mix, crushed**
½ **teaspoon salt**
½ **teaspoon garlic powder**
⅛ **teaspoon pepper**
½ **teaspoon paprika**

Preheat oven to 450°F. Puncture chicken skin with fork. Brush chicken with juice. Spray a nonstick pan with Pam. Combine stuffing and seasonings in a plastic bag; add drumsticks individually and coat lightly. Arrange chicken in single layer in a 9″ × 9″ baking pan. Bake at 450°F for 30 minutes or until crisp and brown. Blot with towel and serve.

*Serves 4.*

## LASAGNA WITH SPINACH

¾ cup chopped onion
1 tablespoon minced fresh garlic
1 tablespoon margarine
1 15-ounce can tomato paste
1 teaspoon salt
¼ teaspoon pepper
1 teaspoon dried oregano
1 teaspoon basil
2 tablespoons chopped fresh parsley
6 lasagna noodles, cooked according to
    package directions
1 pound part-skim mozzarella cheese
1 pound low-fat cottage cheese
2 10-ounce packages frozen spinach,
    defrosted and drained

In a small saucepan, cook onion and garlic in a tablespoon of margarine 3–4 minutes or until soft, stirring often. Stir in tomato paste, salt, pepper, oregano, and basil. Lower heat and simmer for 15–20 minutes.

Heat oven to 350°F. Place three of the noodles in an 11¾″ × 7½″ × 1¾″ baking dish. Top with about one-third of the sauce, then add one-third of the mozzarella and one-third of the cottage cheese. Spread spinach evenly over cheese.

Top spinach with another third each of sauce, mozzarella, and cottage cheese. Top cheeses with remaining noodles and with remaining third of sauce, mozzarella, and cottage cheese.

Bake 30 minutes at 350°F, until cheese is brown and bubbly. Let stand 10 minutes before cutting into squares.

*Serves 8.*

## DRESSING FOR CABBAGE

1⅔ tablespoons sugar
1 teaspoon salt
2 tablespoons oil
3⅓ tablespoons vinegar

Mix ingredients and chill.

*Serves 1-2.*

## FRESH GREEN BEANS PARMESAN

1 teaspoon salt
4 ounces fresh green beans, washed
and trimmed
1½ teaspoons margarine
⅛ teaspoon garlic powder
1½ teaspoons grated Parmesan cheese

Add salt to ½ cup water and bring to a boil. Add beans and cook until green and crisp, 5-7 minutes. In separate pan, melt margarine; add garlic powder and cheese. Pour over cooked beans.

*Serves 1.*

## STIR-FRIED BROCCOLI

    8 ounces broccoli
    ½ slice ginger
    ½ teaspoon dry sherry
    ¼ teaspoon salt
    ¼ teaspoon sugar
    2 tablespoons water
    1½ teaspoons soy sauce (light or dark)
    ½ teaspoon cornstarch
    1½ teaspoons water
    2 tablespoons broth (chicken or beef)

Wash and drain broccoli. Cut into two parts—flowerettes and stems. Cut flowerettes into small pieces. Peel rough parts from stems, and cut stems in quarters; then cut quarters into smaller slices on the diagonal.

Combine sherry, salt, sugar, and water in a large saucepan. Separately, mix soy sauce, water, and broth; dissolve cornstarch in this mixture. Add cornstarch mixture to sherry mixture. Heat, and add broccoli to broth; cook 1–2 minutes, stirring quickly. Add sauce to broccoli and broth, and cover 30 seconds. Remove cover, stir again, and cook uncovered 30 or more seconds. Broccoli should be emerald green.

*Serves 1.*

# 10
# Step 7:
# The *I-Quit-Smoking Diet* Activity Plan

Upon quitting smoking, your final step to ensure weight stabilization is to increase your level of activity through some form of exercise. We are continually bombarded with information about the positive ramifications, both physical and psychological, of exercise. But for many, the word *exercise* alone is enough to make their muscles ache! Many know they "should" exercise but hate the thought of it. Hopefully, the information and suggestions offered here will help alleviate some of those feelings.

Just think—if you smoked a pack a day and it took you five minutes to smoke each cigarette, you have spent 100 minutes or 1½ hours a day smoking. If you substitute just 30 minutes of activity each day, you get to feel healthy and decrease the odds of adding extra pounds.

Activity is one way you can meet the important goals of taking care of your emotional self and planning things that make you feel good about you. It can also act as a diversionary tactic; that is, when you have a craving, and you know it's not stemming from an emotional issue, but rather from a habitual stimuli, doing something physical will take your mind off food. While you're active, it's hard to light up or eat. Beginning an activity plan also can be one more positive step in taking control of your life.

Upon quitting smoking, our bodies begin the healing process quite quickly. Exercise, if implemented regularly, can dramatically increase this healing process, and it does not have to be an exercise program that resembles training in the Marines Corps! Exercise can help you in some of the same ways smoking has "helped" you, but without the negative consequences. Here are some of the benefits a regular activity program can offer, in contrast to the effects of smoking:

| While You Smoke | While You Exercise |
| --- | --- |
| • Carbon monoxide is inhaled and replaces oxygen in the blood cells, leading to tiredness and less endurance. | • Blood volume increases, which increases the number of oxygen-carrying cells (you get more energy). |
| • Blood pressure increases because blood vessels are restricted. | • Blood pressure decreases because blood vessels are open and pliable. |
| • Gas exchange and breathing capacity decrease because of too much mucus in the lungs. | • The diffusion of respiratory gases and breathing capacity increase, causing the walls of the lungs to be more supple. |

| | |
|---|---|
| • Atherosclerosis occurs (that is, plaque builds up in the arteries), which is of serious concern in the development of heart disease because the reduced size of the artery increases the pressure of blood against the artery walls. | • The number of HDLs (high-density lipoproteins) increases. HDLs are sometimes called the "good cholesterol," because they carry the plaque away from the arteries, thus cleaning them out and reducing the chance of a stroke or heart attack. |
| • Nicotine increases the heart rate, putting greater strain on the heart. | • The heart rate decreases because the contractions become stronger, and are able to pump more blood to the body with fewer beats. (There is less "fluttering" feeling.) |
| • Circulation to the limbs decreases, which may cause cramps, numbness, and tingling. | • Circulation increases, which develops auxiliary peripheral circulation, allowing blood to flow to arms and legs even though other normal routes may be blocked (leading to less fatigue while walking). |
| • Air sacs in the lungs are destroyed, decreasing lung capacity. | • The blood supply increases, so less air remains in the lungs and there is less gasping for breath. |
| • Density of the bones diminishes, weakening them. | • Density of the bones increases, leading to fewer broken bones and fewer problems with bones in old age. |
| • Metabolism increases slightly, but with major negative side effects. | Metabolism increases greatly, with major positive side effects. |

The following list shows the benefits of regular exercise, divided into categories. When you need a quick bit of encouragement, just turn to this section.

1. *Benefits to coronary circulation:*
   - Increased collateral circulation, helping veins and arteries circulate blood throughout the body
   - Lowered heart rate at rest and at work
   - Increased size of coronary blood vessels
   - More protection during extreme activity or emotional stress
   - Peripheral circulation to muscles, increasing the size of the muscle fiber, which builds strength and endurance

2. *Benefits to blood pressure:*
   - Decreased rhythmic contractions of the heart (especially in the ventricles) following each beat as the blood is brought to and from the heart chamber
   - Possible counteraction of effects of high-salt diet (but be wise and use salt moderately)

3. *Benefits to the blood:*
   - Reduced serum uric acid, which is a primary cause of gout and a possible contributor to coronary artery disease
   - Increased total blood volume, due to the increased plasma level
   - Improved blood flow through veins and arteries

4. *Benefits to fat (lipid) metabolism:*
   - Increased concentration of high-density lipoproteins, which help carry plaque away from the arteries and divert cholesterol to the liver for breakdown and excretion

- Increased metabolism, so that after exercise, the body continues to burn calories more efficiently for three hours (see section on walking)
- Reduction of triglycerides (fatty deposits formed by acids) during exercise

5. *Benefits to pulmonary (lung) function:*
    - Improved endurance of respiratory muscles— very important in preventing chronic pulmonary disease, which can be a direct consequence of smoking
    - Improved total lung volume
    - Improved lung capacity after exercise is completed
    - Improved capacity for oxygen transport

6. *Benefits in cancer prevention:*
    - According to several studies, correlation with lower incidence of cancer (no proven cause-and-effect relationship)

7. *Benefits in reducing stress:*
    - Improved ability to relax
    - Decreased muscular tension
    - A direct healthy outlet to vent frustration

8. *Feeling good!*

# CHOOSING AN ACTIVITY THAT SUITS YOU

Before you decide to seek these benefits through an activity program, check with your physician. Also explore your possibilities. For example, how do you feel about physical activity? What kind of sports would be best suited to your lifestyle and body type? To get a better idea of the kind of activity that will best suit you, take a few minutes to complete the following activity profile. Answer each statement by circling the number that most closely indicates how you feel. There are six categories to consider: image, enjoyment, appearance, discipline, exercise, and activity. Each of these traits refer to how you currently feel about your activity program or lack of one. Some of the information you receive from this questionnaire may not be news to you, but some new information will emerge, also. This information, whether old or new, is another tool in helping you determine what kind of activity plan will suit you most efficiently over the long term. Your answers will ultimately help you in assessing what kind of activity you are willing to incorporate into your life.

## ACTIVITY PROFILE

|  | Agree | Disagree |
|---|---|---|
| 1. Basically I am an active person. | 4 | 1 |
| 2. I walk rather than drive whenever possible. | 4 | 1 |
| 3. Exercise is enjoyable. | 4 | 1 |
| 4. When I was a child, my family encouraged me to exercise. | 4 | 1 |
| 5. I exercise more than once a week. | 4 | 1 |
| 6. Exercise is not boring to me. | 4 | 1 |
| 7. The ability to master a fitness program would be an exciting challenge for me. | 4 | 1 |
| 8. I make time to exercise several times a week. | 4 | 1 |
| 9. I consciously plan a time for physical activity. | 4 | 1 |

10. I have a greater sense of well-being after I exercise.    4    1

11. I use stairs rather than elevators or escalators.    4    1

12. I don't make excuses not to exercise.    4    1

13. I have a formal exercise plan that I follow.    4    1

14. I find time every day to do something active.    4    1

15. Maintaining a fitness program would show that I have willpower.    4    1

16. My job involves more movement than sitting.    4    1

17. Looking good is very important to me.    4    1

18. Physically fit people always look better.    4    1

19. I participate in some sport (tennis, aerobics, jogging, swimming) at least once a week.    4    1

20. I don't like looking unfit.    4    1

Now you are ready to interpret your answers. As mentioned previously, there are six categories to consider. The first category is image, and this score will indicate your feelings about being active. We all make judgments when we see people, or ourselves, active. Some people think it's great, while others may find it egotistic, and still others may be ambivalent. Your score in this area will give you an idea of how you feel about being active. The second category is enjoyment, which is somewhat self-explanatory. This score will suggest to you how much you actually enjoy physical activity. You may be surprised at your answer! The third category is appearance. This score can help you determine how important your appearance is to you and whether it will be a motivator. The fourth category, discipline, will clue you in to how disciplined you have been or are about your present physical fitness program. The fifth category, exercise, will give you a reading of the extent to which a regular exercise regime is part of your life. From this, you can determine what changes you may need to consider. The last category is activity, and this score will suggest how active your overall lifestyle is and, again, what changes may be needed.

For each of these categories, fill in the blanks with the number from each statement listed.

**Image** — Add answers from statement 1 _____ plus statement 4 _____ plus statement 9 _____ = _____ (image factor).

**Enjoyment** — Add answers from statement 3 _____ plus statement 6 _____ plus statement 10 _____ = _____ (enjoyment factor).

**Appearance** — Add answers from statement 17 _____ plus statement 18 _____ plus statement 20 _____ = _____ (appearance factor).

**Discipline** — Add answers from statement 7 _____ plus statement 13 _____ plus statement 15 _____ = _____ (discipline factor).

Exercise — Add answers from statement 5 _____ plus statement 8 _____ plus statement 12 _____ plus statement 19 _____ = _____ (exercise factor).

Activity — Add answers from statement 2 _____ plus statement 11 _____ plus statement 14 _____ plus statement 16 _____ = _____ (activity factor).

Here's how to interpret your scores.

# Image

If your image factor is 9 or more, you already think of yourself as an active person. Becoming involved in a regular exercise program will be easy for you.

If you scored 6 or less, you probably picture yourself as inactive. In that case, you will want to begin your exercise program with a very easy program that will give you positive results and will change your image of yourself.

# Enjoyment

If your enjoyment factor is 9 or more, you are lucky enough to already enjoy exercising and are aware that stopping smoking will make exercise even more enjoyable.

If you scored 6 or less, you don't find exercise enjoyable—yet! In this chapter, you'll learn many simple ways to bring more activity into your life that will change your view of exercise.

# Appearance

If your appearance factor is 9 or more, your appearance is important to you, and you are aware of how terrific exercise can make you look.

If you scored 6 or less, you may be more concerned with your health than your looks. Remember that exercise is extremely important to good health.

# Discipline

If your discipline factor is 9 or more, control is very important to you. That may have been one of the reasons you stopped your smoking habit, and exercise will enhance that feeling of self-control.

If you scored 6 or less, try keeping records of the changes you are making in your lifestyle since you have stopped smoking. This will enable you to see how well you are doing and will act as positive reinforcement for those changes.

# Exercise

If your exercise factor is 13 or above, you are to be congratulated. You have already developed a regular exercise program that is working for you.

If you scored 10 or below, you are probably not getting enough exercise. Now is the perfect time to start your program, because now is when you will get the greatest benefits and see the most progress.

# Activity

If your activity factor is 13 or above, you now are active in your daily life. Finding more ways to be active will be enjoyable.

If you scored 10 or below, you probably don't think of

yourself as active. You will be pleasantly surprised that there are many small, relatively painless ways to add a great deal of activity to your daily routine.

# EXERCISE FOR THE EX-SMOKER

Now it's time to begin to create an activity program that will work for you, especially during those first critical weeks of adjustment to physical and psychological changes that result from quitting smoking. The good news is that if you do begin an activity plan, you will feel the positive effects almost immediately. If you are a man over 35 or a woman over 40 who has not been exercising or has joint problems, back problems, or other physical concerns, please consult your doctor before starting any exercise program.

The activity plan in this chapter includes four primary components, which you can adapt to meet your particular needs:

1. A walking program
2. Aerobic activities that will help relieve stress as well as burn calories
3. Optional activities that you can use for stretching and flexibility or just fun
4. Relaxation techniques

For any program to be totally effective, it should consist of strengthening, flexibility, and muscular and cardiovascular endurance. Strengthening exercises make the muscles stronger, firmer, and trimmer; calisthenics and weight lifting are usually the most beneficial ways to do this. Flexibility exercises keep joint movements smooth and allow the joint to move through the greatest range; yoga-type exercises and slow stretching are the best means of keeping the body flexible. Muscular endurance refers to a muscle repeating an action numerous times; sit-ups and push-ups are excellent examples of muscular endurance exercises. Cardiovascular endurance refers to the ability of the heart and the lungs to sustain any activity over a period of time; any activity that is continuous, rhythmic, and uses the large muscle group (arms and legs) develops endurance.

Which category of exercise should you concentrate on while you are stopping smoking and hoping to not gain weight? Cardiovascular or aerobic activities are definitely the best route to go. Aerobic exercise uses body fat as its main source of energy during exercise. In other words, while moving aerobically, your body burns fat. No other form of activity does this as effectively as aerobics. The exercise plan offers flexibility exercises during warm-ups and cool-downs, as well as other activities to develop some strength and endurance. If you find strength and flexibility workouts enjoyable, by all means increase the amount of time you do them. They do burn calories, and all activity has its benefits. Do what feels right for *you*.

Aerobic exercise means "exercise with oxygen." The activity is vigorous enough to require oxygen for all physiological systems to function properly, but not so strenuous that the body has too little oxygen to perform. For aerobic exercise to be beneficial to the heart and lungs, it must meet three conditions:

1. *Frequency:* Whatever plan you choose should be done a minimum of three times per week.
2. *Intensity:* You measure this by taking your pulse rate and making sure it is 70–75 percent of your maximum heart rate.

**3.** *Time involved:* For best results, you need to be active for at least thirty minutes.

When you do aerobic exercise, your pulse rate really tells it all. This pulse or heart rate is your body's barometer of many functions. Just by taking your pulse, you can find out how hard you are working, how many calories you are burning, and how your activity program is progressing. Taking your pulse will enable you to fine-tune your program for maximum results.

Here's how you do it: place your index finger on your Adam's apple. Now move your finger directly to the right or left, pressing gently until you feel a thump-thump (that's your carotid artery). You do not have to press hard. Take your finger away, and try it again several times until you can put your finger right on the artery.

The normal range for a heart rate is about 70–90 beats per minute at rest but can be as high as 200 beats per minute when exercising. The fitter you are, the lower your resting pulse will be and the more difficult it will be to increase your pulse. So your goal is to have a low resting pulse and a significantly higher exercising pulse. You want a low resting pulse because if your resting heart is beating only 60 times per minute rather than 70 times, your heart is doing less work. Therefore it will last longer, and so should you! While you exercise aerobically, the higher exercising pulse is increasing your oxygen intake and building up the heart's endurance. This enables it to work less while resting.

To figure out your maximum heart rate, use this simple formula:

**1.** Subtract your age from the number 220.

2. Multiply the difference by .70. This number will be your lower exercise-level heart rate.
3. Repeat step 1 and then multiply the difference by .75. This number will be your upper exercise-level heart rate.

To summarize:

$$(220 - \text{Age}) \times .70 = \text{Lower Exercise Heart Rate}$$

For example, if you are 30 years old, your computation would look like this:

$$220 - 30 = 190$$

$190 \times .70 = 133$     133 beats per minute would be your lower exercise heart rate.

$190 \times .75 = 142$ (rounded off)     142 beats per minute would be your upper exercise heart rate.

Exercising at 70–75 percent of capacity allows you to burn fat and calories under conditions you can maintain safely. The longer you continue an activity, the more calories you will burn and the better you will feel. To make sure you are exercising within these guidelines, take your pulse for 15 seconds right after exercising, and then multiply the number by 4. Compare the result to your target heart rate, or use the guidelines for a 15-second count in the chart on the next page.

As you begin to exercise, you may find yourself slightly out of breath. Don't worry; this is normal. If you can carry on a normal conversation, you are working at an appropriate intensity. If you have difficulty talking, slow down a bit. Longer and slower is more beneficial than quicker and faster.

## TARGET HEART RATES

| Age | 70 Percent of Capacity | | 75 Percent of Capacity | |
|-----|-----------------|-------------------|-----------------|-------------------|
| | Beats per Minute | Beats per 15 Seconds | Beats per Minute | Beats per 15 Seconds |
| 25–29 | 135 | 34 | 144 | 36 |
| 30–34 | 132 | 33 | 140 | 35 |
| 35–39 | 129 | 32 | 136 | 34 |
| 40–44 | 126 | 31 | 133 | 33 |
| 45–49 | 124 | 31 | 129 | 32 |
| 50–54 | 122 | 30 | 125 | 31 |
| 55–59 | 119 | 29 | 121 | 30 |
| 60–64 | 117 | 29 | 118 | 29 |
| 65–69 | 114 | 28 | 114 | 28 |

NOTE: This is the rate that would be your "target." Work at a pace that you feel comfortable with—don't kill yourself to get to the "magic number." Just keep the number in mind as a goal.

## Clothes

When you exercise, wear comfortable clothing; the material should be cotton because it allows your skin to "breathe." If you are exercising outside, dress in light layers so you can shed some if you get too warm. Sweats are terrific for cooler weather, and cotton shorts and T-shirts are fine in warmer weather. If you work out in a health club, do not feel you have to spend hundreds of dollars on matching leotards and tights. Wear what's right for you.

## Shoes

Shoes are the single most important piece of equipment you should invest in. If you are walking, a good comfortable pair of shoes is fine, but if you plan to do extensive walking, running, or aerobic dancing, you should buy shoes that fit properly and are specifically made for the activity. The shoe should have a good arch support and cushioning for the bottoms of your feet. To allow for movement, there should be at least ¼–½ inch between your big toe and the tip of the shoe. The shoe should be made of material that breathes, such as leather, canvas, or nylon mesh.

When you try on the shoes, walk, run, or dance in them right in the store. If you aren't comfortable immediately, you probably never will be. The old theory of "they just need breaking in" never applies to exercise shoes.

## Warm-Ups

Begin any exercise period with some kind of warm-up. A five- to ten-minute routine helps gradually increase circulation, pulse, respiration, and body temperature. Walking slowly is often helpful. After you begin to feel warm, you can do a few basic stretches.

To stretch the lower back and upper legs, with knees slightly bent, bend over at the waist, and hang loosely for about 20 seconds (*no bouncing*). Don't try to touch your toes; just hang.

To stretch the front of the legs, place one hand on the wall for support, then grab and hug the opposite knee to your chest. Alternate legs. You can also do this lying down. Lie on the floor with legs outstretched. Keep one leg straight, and hug the opposite knee to your chest . . .

really hug it! Then alternate legs. Repeat each stretch five times.

To stretch the calf and ankle area, face a wall, and place both hands on the wall. Move your feet about three feet away from the wall, and press your heel to the ground. You should feel a gentle stretch just above the heel.

## Cool-Downs

After you've exercised, it is important to cool down in order to allow the body to gradually return to normal. If you stop suddenly, you may become light-headed and feel cramping in your legs. The easiest way to cool down is simply to repeat the warm-ups for five to ten minutes as well as to do the relaxation techniques that begin on page 164.

## Progress

When starting any exercise program, remember the three Cs:

1. Use your *Common sense.* If any activity hurts or doesn't feel right for you, discontinue it. "Feeling the burn" is not my philosophy!
2. Be *Consistent.* The real benefits of any activity are usually felt after about four weeks of regular (three to four times per week) activity. So keep it up!
3. Be *Conservative.* A slower start will result in fewer injuries, less frustration, and a greater feeling of accomplishment. Your body will tell you when to increase the intensity and duration of your activity, and if you listen to your body, you should progress naturally and easily.

# WALKING PROGRAM

Anytime you make major changes in your life, such as quitting smoking, it's best not to try to make huge changes in other areas. For most of us, several big changes are just too much to expect, and such schemes are bound to end up in defeat. This is especially true about starting an exercise plan. I once joined a health club and told myself I should go every day for at least 1½ hours. I think I lasted three visits!

So begin slowly and realistically. I suggest you start by walking. No fancy, complicated, expensive program—just walk. Walking is easy, accessible, requires no expensive equipment (except a good pair of comfortable shoes), and is something you already know how to do. Also, you don't have to commit huge amounts of time for it to be beneficial. Usually about 20–30 minutes three or four times a week is great (feel free to do more if you wish). Also, you can walk alone or with a friend and at any time you choose, day or evening.

Walking a mile in 15 minutes burns about 7 calories per minute or 105 calories per mile. After you have finished walking, you are still burning calories quickly for about three hours. So just walking 10–12 minutes in the morning, or maybe taking a longer route on the way to work and then repeating that 10–12 minutes later in the day, will allow you to easily burn off over 700 calories per week without changing anything else. Not only that, you are improving your physical health.

Before or after exercise, it is a good idea to do some deep breathing. This can serve as a warm-up or a cooldown. (Also see pages 156–57.) Stand or sit comfortably with feet apart. Close your eyes, and let your head bend slowly forward. Slowly inhale through your nose, feeling your lungs filling, gently pushing all the air into your stomach, and feeling your abdomen expanding. Slowly exhale through your mouth. Repeat this exercise four times. (If you find yourself feeling dizzy, do not continue.) When you are relaxed, either begin your walking program or go on with whatever your day offers. Feel free to do this exercise throughout the day. It can be quite relaxing and helpful in reducing daily tension.

# AEROBIC AND OPTIONAL ACTIVITIES

After you are comfortable with a daily walking plan and notice you are feeling pretty good, it might be time to consider adding more to your activity plan. The following outline for a three-week plan includes increased aerobics combined with suggestions for other activities. These activities can include stretching, weight lifting, working out on exercise machines, or just taking the stairs instead of the elevator. As always, choose activities you think you will really do.

The three-week plan that follows is a guideline. It offers a great deal of room for choosing the activities you feel will be right for your physical level and your lifestyle. It offers daily activities, but exercising three or four times per week is fine, too. After the three-week plan is a chart that lists 50 different activities to choose from. As always, feel free to add any other.

# DIET ACTIVITY PLAN

## Week 1

Sunday — 200-calorie activity(ies). These may be divided into different periods throughout the day.

Monday — Aerobic activity, 25–35 minutes. (See 100-calorie chart for suggestions.)

Tuesday — 200-calorie activity(ies).

Wednesday — Aerobic activity, 25–35 minutes.

Thursday — 200-calorie activity(ies).

Friday — Aerobic activity, 25–35 minutes.

Saturday — 200-calorie activity(ies).

## Week 2

Sunday — 200-calorie activity(ies).

Monday — Aerobic activity, 30–35 minutes.

Tuesday — 200-calorie activity(ies).

Wednesday — Aerobic activity, 30–35 minutes.

Thursday — 200-calorie activity(ies).

Friday — Aerobic activity, 30–35 minutes.

Saturday — 200-calorie activity(ies).

## Week 3

Sunday — 200-calorie activity(ies).

Monday — Aerobic activity, 35–45 minutes.

Tuesday — 200-calorie activity(ies).

Wednesday — Aerobic activity, 35–45 minutes.

Thursday — 200-calorie activity(ies).

Friday — Aerobic activity, 35–45 minutes.

Saturday — 200-calorie activity(ies).

# 100-CALORIE ACTIVITIES

| WOMAN, 125 POUNDS | | MAN, 150 POUNDS | |
|---|---|---|---|
| Activity | Minutes to Burn 100 Calories | Activity | Minutes to Burn 100 Calories |
| Running or jogging (10 mph) | 8 | Running or jogging (10 mph) | 6 |
| Sit-ups and push-ups | 8 | Sit-ups and push-ups | 6 |
| Basketball—vigorous | 10 | Basketball—vigorous | 8 |
| Cycling (13 mph) | 10 | Cycling (13 mph) | 8 |
| Backpacking | 11 | Backpacking | 9 |
| Jogging—medium | 11 | Downhill skiing (10 mph) | 9 |
| Weight lifting—heavy | 11 | Jogging—medium | 9 |
| Downhill skiing (10 mph) | 12 | Squash or handball | 9 |
| Squash or handball | 12 | Weight lifting—heavy | 9 |
| Aerobics—heavy | 13 | Aerobics—heavy | 10 |
| Calisthenics—heavy | 13 | Calisthenics—heavy | 10 |
| Jazzercise—heavy | 13 | Jazzercise—heavy | 10 |
| Racquetball—social | 13 | Racquetball—social | 10 |
| Climbing (100 feet/hour) | 14 | Climbing (100 feet/hour) | 11 |
| Football—touch | 15 | Football—touch | 12 |
| Jogging—slow | 15 | Jogging—slow | 12 |
| Water skiing | 15 | Water skiing | 12 |
| Disco dancing | 17 | Tennis | 13 |
| Tennis | 17 | | |

## 100-CALORIE ACTIVITIES *(cont'd)*

### WOMAN, 125 POUNDS

| Activity | Minutes to Burn 100 Calories |
|---|---|
| Ditch digging—hand | 18 |
| Ice skating (10 mph) | 18 |
| Wood chopping and sawing | 18 |
| Badminton | 20 |
| Horseback trotting | 20 |
| Roller skating | 20 |
| Square dancing | 20 |
| Table tennis | 20 |
| Volleyball | 20 |
| Aerobics—medium | 21 |
| Carpentry—general | 21 |
| Jazzercise—medium | 21 |
| Fencing | 24 |
| Rowing (2.5 mph) | 24 |
| Swimming (0.25 mph) | 24 |
| Walking (3.75 mph) | 24 |
| Calisthenics—light | 26 |
| Housework—cleaning | 26 |

### MAN, 150 POUNDS

| Activity | Minutes to Burn 100 Calories |
|---|---|
| Disco dancing | 14 |
| Ditch digging—hand | 14 |
| Ice skating (10 mph) | 14 |
| Wood chopping and sawing | 14 |
| Badminton | 16 |
| Horseback trotting | 16 |
| Square dancing | 16 |
| Volleyball | 16 |
| Roller skating | 16 |
| Table tennis | 16 |
| Aerobics—medium | 17 |
| Carpentry—general | 17 |
| Jazzercise—medium | 17 |
| Fencing | 19 |
| Rowing (2.5 mph) | 19 |
| Swimming (0.25 mph) | 19 |
| Walking (3.75 mph) | 19 |
| Bowling | 21 |
| Calisthenics—light | 21 |

## 100-CALORIE ACTIVITIES *(cont'd)*

| WOMAN, 125 POUNDS | | MAN, 150 POUNDS | |
|---|---|---|---|
| Activity | Minutes to Burn 100 Calories | Activity | Minutes to Burn 100 Calories |
| Weight lifting—light | 26 | Housework—cleaning | 21 |
| Bowling | 27 | Lawn mowing (hand) | 21 |
| Lawn mowing (hand) | 27 | Weight lifting—light | 21 |
| Golf | 29 | Golf | 23 |
| Lawn mowing (power) | 29 | Lawn mowing (power) | 23 |
| Canoeing (2.5 mph) | 32 | Canoeing (2.5 mph) | 25 |
| Gardening | 33 | Gardening | 26 |
| Aerobics—light | 35 | Aerobics—light | 28 |
| Bicycling (5.5 mph) | 35 | Bicycling (5.5 mph) | 28 |
| Jazzercise—light | 35 | Jazzercise—light | 28 |
| Shuffleboard/skeet | 35 | Shuffleboard/skeet | 28 |
| Walking (2.5 mph) | 35 | Walking (2.5 mph) | 28 |
| Billiards | 52 | Billiards | 42 |

# RELAXATION TECHNIQUES

Every good exercise program should include some relaxation techniques. They are beneficial any time of day but are especially good right after a good workout.

Relaxation techniques can be looked upon as "soothing exercise" because you are using your body, your heart, lungs, and muscles. You can use relaxation exercise after regular exercise, during periods of stress, and as an alternative to smoking. You have already found the benefits of deep breathing, and should feel very comfortable practicing this technique. Yoga can also be used as a method of relaxation.

The key to reaping the greatest benefits, especially immediately after you've stopped smoking, is to set aside a time each day for yourself to relax. Plan to spend about 15-20 minutes relaxing. You will be amazed at how refreshed you feel, and that wonderful feeling will act as a reason to do it regularly.

Here's a basic approach: find a quiet place with a comfortable chair, and wear comfortable clothing. Begin by deep breathing. After deep breathing, tense and relax the muscles of your body for 2-3 seconds, until you finally feel totally relaxed.

1. Tense one leg, beginning with your toes, continuing up to your thigh. After holding for 2-3 seconds, relax that leg. Repeat with the other leg.
2. Tighten your abdominal muscles by pressing your navel to your spine, and hold for 2-3 seconds. Relax.
3. Tense the muscles in your chest by pushing downward for 2-3 seconds. Then relax 2-3 seconds.
4. Tighten the muscles of the back and shoulders by pressing back, and hold for 2-3 seconds. Release.
5. Tighten the muscles in your right arm by bending one elbow and making a tight fist. Hold for 2-3 seconds. Repeat with the other arm, then relax.

6. Tense the muscles in your neck for 2-3 seconds. Release for 2-3 seconds.
7. Tighten every muscle in your face for 2-3 seconds. Then relax 2-3 seconds.

Now, sit quietly for a few minutes, enjoying the feelings of peace and tranquility.

## Mental Imagery or Visualization

Mental imagery or visualization is an effective way to use all your senses to relax, to create images of something you would like, and to rehearse positive behaviors. Use the following exercise like a mini vacation, and use your imagination to visualize yourself in that situation. This technique can be used with anything you find pleasurable—except smoking!

> Picture yourself walking along the beach, digging your toes into the warm sand. It is early morning, the sun is shining brightly, the lake is crystal clear, and you can smell the water, the sand, and the grasses. You sit by the water; the sand is warm, and the water is washing up over your ankles. A gentle wind moves the sand and water around you. You lie down and look up at the clouds floating by, and you begin to float up toward the clouds, feeling completely weightless, moving effortlessly as a cloud would move. You breathe in, feeling the warmth of the air around you, and are feeling very relaxed. You slowly, reluctantly float down to the beach, landing as a feather would land. Slowly open your eyes, and feel energy flowing through your entire body.

You can use visualization as a "rehearsal" for the situations that bring the greatest desire for a cigarette or a snack. Studies have suggested that by visualizing just one time, you increase your chances for success by 40 percent. If you visualize 20 times, you are 60 percent more likely to achieve your desired goal, and if you visualize using all your senses, your chances for success rise to 75 percent! This may seem a bit farfetched, but think about the things you have achieved in your life. Usually, the goals we *really* want are ones we have thought about in great detail. For example, I have spent the last five years seeing myself writing a book and getting it published. Need I say more?

To visualize, you do not have to sit with white candles and chant a special prayer! If you want to do this, that's fine, but visualization can take on any form you choose. I do it in bed before I go to sleep. Some people do it in the car; others while they ride the train to work. Whatever you feel comfortable with is OK.

To begin, pick several concrete situations that you would like to see yourself handling differently. You might want to begin by choosing situations where you might be likely to grab a cigarette or a munchie. Jot them down. For example, here are 10 common stressful situations for an ex-smoker:

1. Having a cup of coffee
2. After a meal
3. Socializing with friends
4. Driving the car
5. Watching television
6. Playing cards
7. At work
8. Feeling frustrated
9. Waiting for someone
10. After a movie

Pick the situation that bothers you the most. Let's say it's having a cup of coffee. Sit down and totally relax, using some of the relaxation techniques already suggested. When you are completely relaxed, with eyes closed, begin imagining yourself sitting with your coffee, without a cigarette and without a doughnut. Smell the coffee, feel the cup in your hands, taste it, check out your surroundings, and be part of the scenario. See yourself relaxed, enjoying your coffee. Note how much better you feel, how much easier you breathe, how much more you can enjoy your surroundings without the cigarette or doughnut. See yourself finishing your coffee and getting on with whatever else you need to complete. Take two or three deep, slow breaths, and open your eyes. You should feel peaceful and relaxed.

You may need to repeat this sequence several times before you feel a change. I usually recommend spending about 10–15 minutes on each situation. This, like anything else that is good in life, does take a bit of practice. Some people think visualization is silly and will never work. But if you keep at it, you will see dramatic results. And it certainly doesn't hurt. You will be amazed at how relaxed and confident you will become when you find yourself feeling good in a particular situation that previously was difficult. The more you handle one situation effectively, the more you will become confident in dealing with unexpected stressful situations.

You can use this kind of mental imagery with any area of your life. Just close your eyes, see how you want to be, have a bit of faith in your inner self, and your chances of achieving your desires will increase.

## Positive Self-Talk or Affirmations

Another way to increase your ability to relax and enjoy success is to pay more attention to your self-talk. Self-talk is the constant inner dialogue we have with ourselves. Many of these thoughts can be roadblocks to achievement. Although most of us are nice to and supportive of the people around us, we are not always as gracious to ourselves. Our "other talk" is warm, supportive, and encouraging, while often our "self-talk" is cold, negative, and deflating.

Like visualization, changing the way you talk to yourself should increase your chances of succeeding and feeling better about yourself. But *you* are the one who has to put these suggestions to work to fit *your* life.

Review the following list of positive affirmations, and pick out the ones that appeal to you. Also feel free to write up some of your own.

- I, __[your name]__, can live a life free from cigarettes.
- I, _____, know I feel much better when I am not smoking.
- I, _____, know food is not the enemy; I can eat normal foods and not gain weight.
- I, _____, deserve to be successful in whatever I do.
- I, _____, am ready to put my past behind me and start anew.
- I, _____, really like myself, and so do others.
- I, _____, know I have a variety of feelings, and they are all OK.
- I, _____, know that when I exercise, I feel great.
- I, _____, know that I deserve free time and fun.
- I, _____, know that the person who is in charge of my life is *me*.

When your list is completed, take a few minutes a day to say it out loud. Even if you do not feel your words to be true, keep going. It won't be long before you start feeling that what you say is possible.

# 11
# Conclusion

If you combine education, emotional awareness, a sensible eating plan, and an activity plan you can live with, you should be able to see and experience how a smoke-free life does not have to include extra pounds. Throughout your growth, remember to continue to know yourself and listen to your inner voice. It is there to guide you into being the best you possibly can.

Also, feel free to check out the bibliography that follows. It lists books I have found interesting and easy to read. Often books can be a tremendously helpful source of support and encouragement.

Good luck to you always, and remember: *quitting smoking and gaining weight never have to go hand in hand!*

# Bibliography

For help in the quit-smoking process, contact your local American Lung Association and the American Cancer Society. They have loads of free pamphlets that can be extremely helpful while quitting. Two from the American Lung Association are:

"Freedom from Smoking in 20 Days"
"A Lifetime of Freedom from Smoking"

Two from the American Cancer Society are:

"Strategic Withdrawal from Cigarette Smoking"
"7 Day Plan to Help You Stop Smoking Cigarettes"

## NUTRITION RESOURCES

Brody, Jane. *Jane Brody's Good Food Book.* New York: W. W. Norton & Co., 1985.

————. *Jane Brody's Nutrition Book*. New York: Bantam, 1981.

Hamilton, Eva May, and Eleanor Noss Whitney. *Nutrition: Concepts and Controversies*. St. Paul, MN: West Publishing Co., 1979.

Kraus, Barbara. *Dictionary of Calories and Carbohydrates*. New York: New American Library, 1973.

Mayer, Jean. *A Diet for Living*. New York: David McKay, 1975.

Whitney, Eleanor Noss, and Eva May Hamilton. *Understanding Nutrition*. St. Paul, MN: West Publishing Co., 1987.

Wurtman, Judith J. *Eating Your Way Through Life*. New York: Raven Press, 1979.

# EXERCISE AND RELAXATION RESOURCES

Bailey, Covert. *Fit or Fat*. Boston: Houghton Mifflin, 1977.

Benson, Herbert. *The Relaxation Response*. New York: Morrow, 1975.

Cooper, Kenneth. *The New Aerobics*. New York: M. Evans & Co., 1970.

Denning, Melita and Osborne Phillips, *Creative Visualization*. St. Paul, MN: Llewellyn New Times, 1985.

Fixx, James F. *The Complete Book of Running.* New York: Random House, 1977.

Jacobsen, Edmund. *Progressive Relaxation.* Chicago: University of Chicago Press, 1938.

Whitney, Eleanor Noss and Eva May Hamilton, *Understanding Nutrition.* St. Paul, MN: West Publishing Co., 1987.

Zohman, Lenore. "Beyond Diet: Exercise Your Way to Fitness and Heart Health." Pamphlet, free from Mazola Nutrition Information Service, Dept. ZD-NYT, Box 307, Coventry, CT 06238.

# SELF-HELP RESOURCES

Burns, David D. *The New Mood Therapy.* New York: Morrow, 1980.

Buscaglia, Leo. *Living, Loving and Learning.* Thorofare, NJ: Slack, 1981.

Chernin, Kim. *The Obsession.* New York: Harper & Row, 1981.

Ferguson, Tom. *The Smoker's Book of Health.* New York: G. P. Putnam's Sons, 1987.

Helmstetter, Shad. *What to Say When You Talk to Yourself.* Scottsdale, AZ: Grindle Press, 1986.

Le Shan, Eda. *Winning the Losing Battle (Why I'll Never Be Fat Again.* New York: Thomas Y. Crowell, 1979.

Ogle, Jane. *The Stop Smoking Diet*. New York: M. Evans & Co., 1981.

Orbach, Susie. *Fat Is a Feminist Issue*. New York: Berkley Books, 1978, 1982.

Peck, M. Scott. *The Road Less Traveled*. New York: Simon & Schuster, 1978.

Roth, Geneen. *Feeding the Hungry Heart*. New York: Bobbs-Merrill, 1982.

Sheeley, Gail. *Pathfinders*. New York: Bantam, 1982.

Solomon, Neil. *Stop Smoking, Lose Weight*. New York: Putnam, 1981.